THE BRITISH EMPIRE AND THE GREAT DIVISIONS OF THE GLOBE

Also available from Living Book Press

Elementary Geography (Geography Reader Book 1) - Charlotte Mason
Home Geography for Primary Grades - C.C. Long
Outdoor Geography - Herbert Hatch
Marvels of the Occident - Richard Halliburton
Marvels of the Occident - Richard Halliburton
Secrets of the Universe - Paul Fleisher
Marco Polo - Manuel Komroff
The Wonderland of Nature - Nuri Mass
A Book of Golden Deeds - Charlotte Yonge
　　...and many, many more!

Visit us at www.livingbookpress.com or search for "Living Book Press" on amazon.com

The British Empire and the Great Divisions of the Globe

CHARLOTTE M. MASON

GEOGRAPHY READER BOOK 2

This edition published 2019
By Living Book Press
147 Durren Rd, Jilliby, 2259

Copyright © Living Book Press, 2019

ISBN: 978-1-925729-66-5 (softcover)
        978-1-922619-58-7 (hardcover)

All rights reserved. No part of this publication may be reproduced, stored in a retrieval system, or transmitted in any other form or means – electronic, mechanical, photocopying, recording or otherwise, without the prior permission of the copyright owner and the publisher or as provided by Australian law.

 A catalogue record for this book is available from the National Library of Australia

CONTENTS

1. THE SEAS AND SHORES OF EUROPE. — 3
2. THE SEAS AND SHORES OF EUROPE. PART II. — 5
3. COUNTRIES OF EUROPE. — 8
4. PLAINS AND MOUNTAINS OF EUROPE. — 12
5. PLAINS AND MOUNTAINS OF EUROPE. PART II. — 15
6. RIVERS OF EUROPE. — 18
7. THE BRITISH ISLES. — 22
8. THE BRITISH ISLES. PART II. — 24
9. THE CRUISE OF THE SEAGULL. — 27
10. THE CRUISE OF THE SEAGULL. PART II. — 30
11. ROUND NORTH BRITAIN. — 32
12. THE OCEAN SHORES. — 36
13. THE PRINCIPALITY. — 39
14. THE WESTERN HORN. — 43
15. FROM JOHN O'GROAT'S TO LAND'S END. — 46
16. FROM JOHN O'GROATS TO LAND'S END. PART II. — 50
17. FROM JOHN O'GROAT'S TO LAND'S END. PART III. — 54
18. FROM JOHN O'GROAT'S TO LAND'S END. PART IV. — 57
19. IRELAND. — 63
20. IRELAND. PART II. — 65
21. FRANCE. — 70
22. SPAIN AND PORTUGAL. — 75
23. ITALY. — 79
24. SWITZERLAND. — 83
25. GERMANY. — 88
26. HOLLAND. — 91
27. SWEDEN AND NORWAY. — 95
28. RUSSIA. — 100
29. RUSSIA. PART II. — 103

30	ASIA.	106
31	ASIA. PART II.	108
32	PERSIA.	112
33	ARABIA.	115
34	OUR INDIAN EMPIRE.	119
35	OUR INDIAN EMPIRE. PART II.	123
36	OUR INDIAN EMPIRE. PART III.	127
37	THE CELESTIAL EMPIRE.	129
38	THE CELESTIAL EMPIRE. PART II.	133
39	AFRICA.	136
40	AFRICA. PART II.	140
41	AFRICA. PART III.	145
42	THE NEW WORLD.	149
43	NORTH AMERICA.	153
	THE WEST INDIES	155
44	THE DOMINION OF CANADA.	157
45	THE DOMINION OF CANADA. PART II.	162
46	SOUTH AMERICA.	168
47	THE GREAT SOUTH LAND.	173
	NEW ZEALAND.	176
	POLYNESIA.	177

EDITORS NOTE.

Charlotte Mason wrote this book in a time very different from ours. It is fascinating to read about the cities and countries as they were a little over one hundred years ago.

If you are familiar with any of the locations described in this book you will notice how much has changed in the ways people travel, the industries of areas, and how people make their living. Another thing that has changed a lot since this book was written is our understanding other cultures. Because travel was so time consuming and expensive many of the descriptions of distant lands and people included in the book come from the observations and writing of others. Viewed with today's understanding some of these descriptions were ignorant, wildly inaccurate and offensive. Ms. Mason went against the feeling of the day with respect to education and believed that every child, no matter their background, was capable of learning and understanding. Had she had the opportunity to meet many of the people negatively described by others I have no doubt that she would have believed they too were far better than the descriptions that were originally used.

In keeping with what I believe Ms. Mason would have desired I have deleted a few phrases from the book that were particularly negative toward entire groups of people.

Footnotes of what was changed have not been included as I believe some of the original descriptions would only serve to diminish the respect in which Ms. Mason and her work are held.

Anthony
Living Book Press

PREFACE.

Children should be familiar with the Map of the World before the geography of any division of the earth's surface is studied in detail, and perhaps the year in "Standard III." is a good time in which to lay this foundation for geographical knowledge.

"The situation of the several parts of the earth is better learned by one day's conversing with a map, than by merely reading the description of their situation a hundred times over in a book of geography."—Dr. Watts, 'On the Improvement of the Mind.'

It is hoped this little book may prove of use as a "Child's Guide to the Map of the World." The object of the reading lessons is to associate ideas of interest with the various States and regions of the world, with the situation of which the children are made familiar; and, at the same time, to convey in simple language a few of the leading facts and principles of Geography.

The parts of the British Empire are treated in detail; these, being widely scattered, are best studied in connection with the divisions of the earth to which they belong.

It is proposed that only the chapters relating to the British Empire should be studied for examination purposes, the rest of the book being read by the class to promote intelligence in their special work.

C. M. M

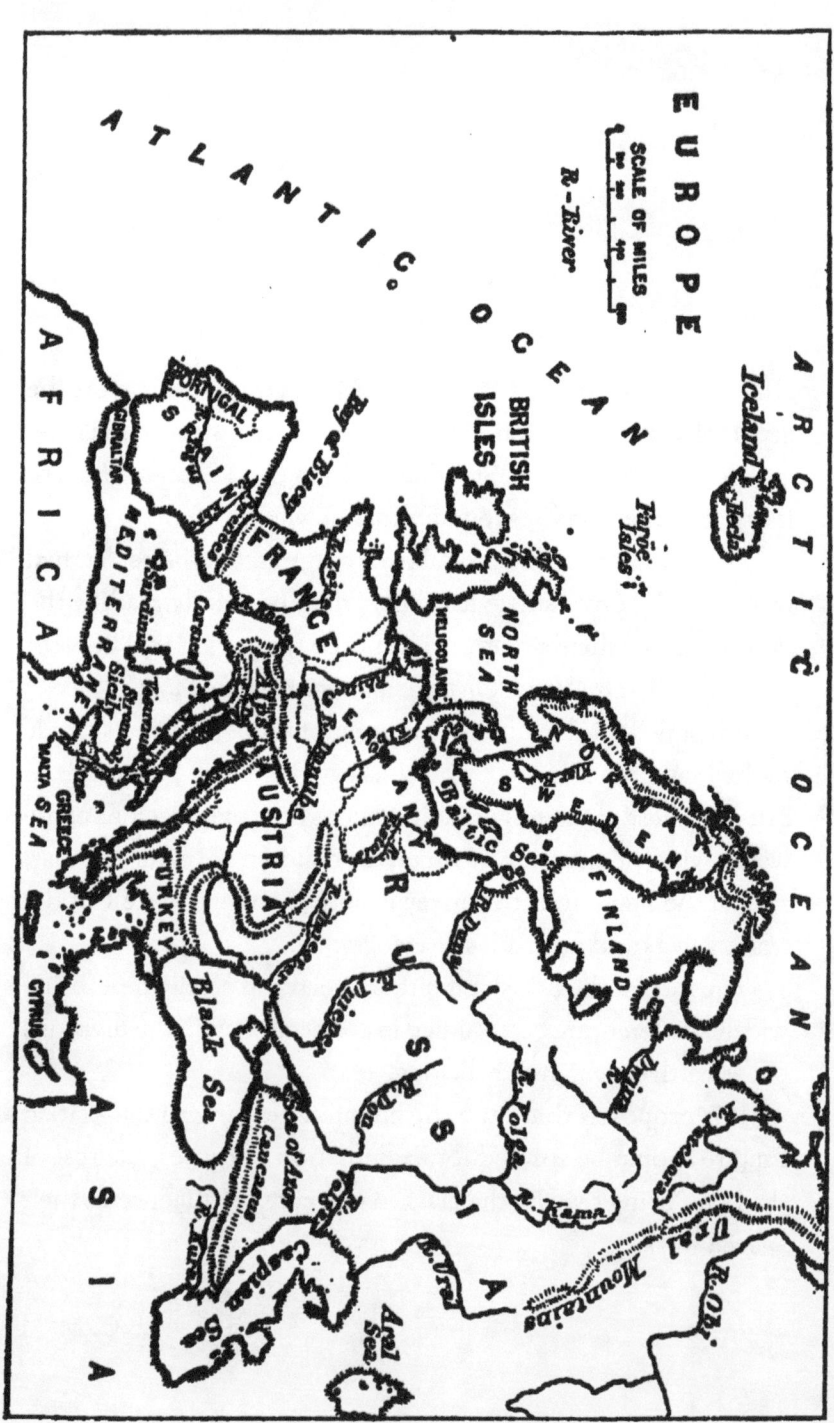

LESSON I.
THE SEAS AND SHORES OF EUROPE.[1]

The seas which bound Europe are branches of the Atlantic, excepting on the north, where the cold waters of the Arctic Ocean wash the coasts. The Atlantic is a much smaller ocean than the Pacific, but it is much more used by the ships which carry on the commerce of the world. It lies between the west coasts of Europe and Africa, and the east coast of America.

The bed of this ocean is unlike that of the Pacific; the high places do not often rise into mountains that appear above water as groups of islands, but they are long, level heights, or plateaus, a great way under water, although much higher than the rest of the ocean bottom. The low parts of the ocean floor lie at a depth of about five miles.

Cables by which telegraphic messages are sent from Europe to America extend from the island of Valencia (off the west coast of Ireland) to Newfoundland, along the floor of the sea at a depth of three miles, in some places, below the surface of the water.

A strange fact about the Atlantic is the movement through its northern basin of a mighty river of warm sea-water. This river is larger than all the fresh water rivers of the world together; and instead of having banks of solid earth, it is walled in on either side by the ocean waters.

This river is the *Gulf Stream*, and its waters keep thus distinct because warm water does not mix readily with cold: it consists of ocean-water which has been heated under the burning sun of the tropics, that is, in the hottest part of the world. This stream flows towards the west, into the Gulf of Mexico, where it is shut in for a while under a hot tropical sun, and when it comes out through

---
[1] For a notice of the general distribution or land and water, see Book I.

the Strait of Florida, it is the broad river of very warm water we have spoken of. Because it has come out of a gulf, it is known as the *Gulf Stream*.

Having swept out of the Strait of Florida, the Gulf Stream flows nearly as far north as Newfoundland; then it crosses the ocean, and one part of the stream passes Britain and Norway. The water loses much of its heat as it flows towards the cold north, but it is still warm enough when it reaches England to keep our harbours from being frozen, and to warm the westerly winds which blow from off the sea over our own country and the maritime countries of Western Europe.

Not only this warm stream, but all the waters which wash the shores of Europe help to make its climate pleasant. Water does not become so hot as dry land in summer, nor so cold in winter. Hence the winds that blow over seas and become filled with watery vapour are cool and pleasant in the summer, and mild and moist in the winter. It is plain, then, that if the winds which reach a country have come across wide waters, that land must have a more pleasant, *temperate* climate than another land which has no sea-breeze to cool it during summer heat, nor warm it during winter cold.

LESSON II.
THE SEAS AND SHORES OF EUROPE.

PART II.

LOOK, now, at a map of Europe; you will find it is broken into by the ocean in a remarkable way,—much more so than any other continent. The Atlantic is an ocean of *inland seas* that enter into the very heart of the land, and most of these are in Europe. To the south, there is the large, blue, beautiful Mediterranean, with the Black Sea and the two small seas connected with it,—the Sea of Marmora and the Sea of Azof; the Archipelago, so full of islands that its name is given to any sea which contains many islands; and the Adriatic. These form a chain of seas, some of which are connected by straits. The burning winds which blow from the African Desert cross the Mediterranean and become somewhat cool and moist before they reach the pleasant lands of Southern Europe. The long name belonging to this sea has a curious history; it means middle of the earth; and was so called because the ancients, to whom a great deal of the world was unknown, thought that the Great Sea, round which lay all the famous countries of the Old World, was indeed the middle of the earth.

Now, look at the west; see how the Bay of Biscay and the English Channel, the Irish Sea and the North Sea, and the Baltic, with the various straits and belts which connect them, break into the very middle of the continent. Notice how, here, as in the south, these inland seas form many peninsulas. In the Mediterranean there are the Spanish peninsula, Italy, and Turkey; and, in the north, the Scandinavian peninsula, and the little northward pointing peninsula of Denmark; to say nothing of Britain, which is not almost, but altogether an island.

Even the cold Arctic serves a kindly purpose; the bitter winds which blow from the icy regions round the pole are a little less keen than if they had come overland. But what is to be said for Eastern Europe? The whole broad continent of Asia stretches between it and the eastern ocean. The consequence is what you might expect, the air is bitterly cold and dry in the winter, and hot and dry in the summer; and never moist and pleasant as are the winds which blow towards Europe across the Atlantic.

The Atlantic with its inland seas benefits Europe in another way; this continent has, for its size, more land bordering on the sea than any other. This long *coast-line* is a great advantage, because countries which have a *seaboard*, or coast-line, can trade far and near with their ships; and as almost every country in Europe has some seaboard, this continent, placed nearly in the middle of the world, is able to carry on a wide *commerce* with the other continents, east and west.

The countries of Europe have not all an equal share in this commerce; those that have much coast-line, like Britain, can most readily become great sea-faring nations. But, for this purpose, the coast must be broken with inlets, which make snug harbours for the ships; an unbroken coast, like that of much of Africa, for instance, is of little use.

Examine the map of Europe to see which countries have the longest and most *indented* coast-lines, and you will find that these either were at one time, or are now, great *maritime*, or sea-going, nations.

By looking at the map you will see that the Atlantic is a highway which carries ships westwards to America, or, southwards, to Africa. By rounding the southern point of Africa, vessels may make for the south and east of Asia. But this, you will see, is a long and roundabout way; if it were not for the little neck of land which separates the Mediterranean from the Red Sea, how easy it would be to sail through these two seas, and out into the Arabian sea, and so across to India! To make this short passage possible, a wonderful piece of work has been finished quite lately; a water-way was dug a hundred miles long, and wide and deep enough for ships to sail in. Then the sea waters rushed in and filled this channel, which is called the Suez Canal, because it cuts through the isthmus of Suez; and ships for India or China, or for any part of the south or east of Asia now go by this most useful canal.

LESSON III.
COUNTRIES OF EUROPE.

A GLANCE at the map shows that the countries of Europe are very unequal in size. The eastern half of the continent is occupied by one huge country which reaches from the Arctic on the north to the Black Sea on the south, and as far west as the Baltic. Our own land only extends through five degrees of latitude, but Russia stretches through thirty degrees from north to south. For this reason, various climates prevail in the different parts of Russia; in the north there are wide frozen plains upon which the sun never rises for weeks during the long Arctic night; while in the south there are warm sunny regions where the vine grows freely.

This large country is an empire. The people are very unlike those of the rest of Europe in their ways, their language, and their religion. St. Petersburg, the capital city, has so many fine houses and other handsome buildings, that it is sometimes called a city of palaces.

To the north-west of Russia are the two countries of Norway and Sweden, which form a peninsula pointing south, and are washed by the sea everywhere except where they join Russia.

The west of Norway is exposed to the strong Atlantic waves; the ocean reaches into the land by many narrow inlets, called fiords, and countless islands fringe the coast.

These countries, also, stretch beyond the Arctic circle into the frigid zone, and have, therefore, long winter nights; but as the people are fond of books, they spend many of these dark hours in study. Stockholm, the capital of Sweden, is built upon several islands joined together by bridges, and is a very clean and beautiful town.

To the south of this is another smaller peninsula, the only one in Europe which points towards the north. With the islands off its eastern coast, it forms the kingdom of Denmark. Copenhagen, the capital, is built upon an island.

The tiny island of HELIGOLAND, which lies off the south-west coast of the peninsula, belongs to Britain.

Still to the south-west, upon the North Bea, are two small, but busy, countries. Holland, the most northerly of these, lies so low that the people are obliged to build strong embankments called dykes to keep the sea from bursting in upon their neat, well-kept towns and carefully tended fields.

Belgium, the small country to the south, is so busy, so full of towns and people, that the whole country looks like one huge city. Beautiful lace and handsome carpets are made in Brussels, its chief town.

These two countries are kingdoms.

The next country to the south-west is a republic. It is the gay and pleasant land of France, with which England had, in old days, many long wars; but English people now go there in crowds to see the country, and Paris, its beautiful capital.

France is washed by the Bay of Biscay on the west, and by the English Channel on the north. The pleasant CHANNEL ISLANDS, Jersey, Guernsey, Alderney, and Sark, belong to England, though they lie off the north coast of France .

Crossing the English Channel, we come to our own country, which, with Scotland to the north, and Ireland (which is an island) to the west, forms the kingdom of GREAT BRITAIN and IRELAND. London, the capital of this kingdom, is the largest and richest city in the world; it does not look so bright and gay as Paris, however, because the smoke from the enormous number of coal fires makes the buildings dingy.

In the south of Europe is a large peninsula, which points southward, and contains the countries of Spain and Portugal. The people of these countries were at one time famous sailors who explored and conquered many lands. Spain and Portugal are kingdoms. A little bit of this large peninsula belongs to England—the rocky fortress of GIBRALTAR, which stands exactly at the opening into the Mediterranean.

The next southern country of Europe is also a peninsula, of a carious shape, something like a boot with a large island off the toe. This is a beautiful land where grapes and oranges grow freely, and where you might live nearly always in the open air. Rome, its capital, was once the greatest city in the world, and had large armies of brave and obedient soldiers who conquered nearly every country known in their day, including our own. But all this glory has long since passed away.

To the south of Sicily are three small islands which belong to Britain—MALTA, GOZO, and COMINO. Malta is the largest and most important of these; it has a delicious climate, and grapes and oranges and other southern fruits grow here as in Italy. British soldiers are stationed here to protect the British merchant ships which trade in the Mediterranean.

The beautiful little country of Switzerland lies, all among the mountains, to the north of this peninsula; it is a republic, inhabited by a brave people. Switzerland is sometimes called the playground of Europe, because crowds of people from other countries go every year to keep holiday among its mountains and lakes.

Separated from Italy by the Adriatic Sea is an other peninsula pointing south, containing two countries. Turkey, the northern of these, is held by the only European nation which is not Christian. Constantinople, its capital, stands on a lovely spot upon the Bosphorus.

The little country of Greece, to the south, was, like Italy, at one time the greatest country in the world. It is pleasant to know that

Saint Paul travelled about here and taught the people, and wrote to some of the towns letters, which we may now read in the Bible.

The rather large island of CYPRUS, which lies in what is called the Levant—that is, the eastern part of the Mediterranean—has fallen quite lately into the occupation of Great Britain. It is a pleasant island, containing many mountains, and large forests of oak and walnut trees. Delicious fruits and various kinds of corn grow on the open plains.

The centre of Europe is occupied by two large empires: to the north-west is Germany, where the people of the various provinces and principalities speak one language, and have, on the whole, a friendly feeling towards each other; and to the south-east is Austria, in which there are two or three countries, between the inhabitants of which little friendly feeling exists, as they speak different languages, and do not belong to one race.

LESSON IV.
PLAINS AND MOUNTAINS OF EUROPE.

BY looking at the map of Europe we may learn a good deal about the appearance of the countries in it. We see which are mountainous, and therefore likely to be beautiful, and whether there are lakes among the mountains to add to their beauty. We see which are the dull, level lands or plains, and if there are lakes in these flat plains. We learn in what part of Europe the mountains lie, and in what directions the various chains run.

The direction of the mountain chains is one of the first things that persons who understand geography notice when they examine a map, because the climate of a country may be a good deal affected by the position of its mountains. These may stand like a huge sheltering wall, to shield the land from the icy north wind, the bitter east, or the burning south; or, while rising as a barrier against all pleasant moisture-laden winds, they may leave the land exposed to the biting blasts off frozen plains. Then, again, the mountains rear their heads so high among the clouds that they cause the watery vapour of which these are composed to drop in frequent showers; so that a mountainous country has generally a good deal of rain, excepting in dry, hot lands, where clouds seldom gather.

We must consider one more fact about mountains. Trace the river lines upon a map to the spot where they begin, and you will find that rivers generally have their sources in mountains. Also, you will notice that several rivers rise in the same range of mountains, and flow in the same general direction until they reach the sea. Look again, and you may see that other rivers rise in these same mountains, and flow in quite an opposite direction, perhaps to empty their waters into another sea. The reason of this is easy to understand. The rain which falls upon a mountain either streams down the slopes in little runlets, or sinks through crevices in the rook deep into the mountain-side. By-and-by the underground crevices become so filled that they can hold no more, and the water is forced out as a *spring*. The waters from many runlets and springs collect and form a *stream*, and the stream makes its way steadily downwards to the lowest land it can reach, and, at last, to the sea, because the sea lies lower than any land. On its way seaward, the mountain stream is joined by many other streams, and fed by many springs, until it becomes a *river*, wide and deep enough in some cases to carry big ships.

Notice two points in this little history of a river: in the first place, runlet, stream, river, are constantly flowing *downwards*. Try to imagine a river rising in land as flat as a table and flowing towards a distant sea, always over quite flat land. You cannot. The water would cease to flow, and would spread into stagnant ponds. A river can only flow so long as it finds some little slope in the land down which it can run. If the slope be great the river rushes along with a headlong course, like a hoop trundled down a hill; the more level the land is, the slower is the current of the rivers, and very sluggish are the streams which creep over wide plains. Knowing that every river must run down a slope, a glance at the map will show in what direction the land slopes—to the west here, to the north there; in whatever direction a river runs from its source to the sea, the general slope of the land must be in that direction.

Notice, in the second place, that it is not upon one side only of a mountain that rain falls and springs rise. If the streams we have been considering have their sources on the southern slope, we may be sure that the same thing takes place on the northern slope also. Now as the streams which rise on the north side cannot possibly flow up the mountains to unite with those which rise on the south side, they must flow down and make for themselves courses in the opposite direction, perhaps towards a far-distant sea. Thus the mountain's ridge divides the streams which rise upon one slope from those which rise upon the other: and, in this way, mountains often form a water-parting; that is, a division or parting between streams which flow in contrary directions. As the direction in which the rivers flow depends thus upon the position of the mountains and the direction of the slope, and as vessels trade upon the rivers, and towns grow up upon their banks, we have here a second reason why the direction of its mountain chains is an important fact in the geography of a continent.

LESSON V.
PLAINS AND MOUNTAINS OF EUROPE.
PART II.

TURNING now to the map of Europe, we notice that the three southern peninsulas are well covered with mountains, while they are marked thickest in Switzerland, the beautiful little country lying to the north of Italy. In fact, the Swiss mountains seem to be the centre of those in the south-west of Europe, and several ranges branch from them into France, Germany, and Austria, as well as into the three peninsulas.

Hungary, a country which forms part of Austria, has a chain of mountains named the Carpathians, curving round its eastern side.

There is also a range, quite away from the rest, stretching from the north to the south of Scandinavia. These are called the Scandinavian Mountains.

All the rest of Europe is very flat, and forms a great plain which takes in the whole of Russia, as well as the countries to the south of the Baltic Sea and the German Ocean. Nearly half of Russia is covered with immense forests, some of them much larger than all the British Isles put together.

Holland, where the sea is kept out by embankments, is one of the lowest parts of the great plain. The other very low part is at the south-east end, round the Caspian Sea; here, a high wind drives the sea-waters over the land; and not only the waters, but the vessels upon them are at times driven upon shore.

In the north of this plain, in Russia, are Ladoga and Onega, the two largest lakes in Europe. Lakes are common in mountain valleys, but sometimes, as here, they fill up the lowest parts of a plain. The long range of Scandinavian Mountains runs close to the Atlantic coast; the sea rushes in between these mountains and fills the narrow valleys which are called *fiords*. The summits of this range are, in the north, covered with perpetual snow and ice, but the sides are clothed with great forests of pine; indeed, these pine forests cover more than three-quarters of the peninsula. There are several large lakes in Sweden, Wener and Wetter being the largest.

The Alps, the highest and grandest of all the mountain ranges of Europe, nearly fill up the little country of Switzerland; whichever way you look, their snowy summits rise, range behind range, further than the eye can follow. We can only get into Italy from Switzerland by crossing a chain of these high Alps, and several passes lead from the one country to the other, as the Splügen Pass, the Simplon Pass, and others. Mont Blanc, the highest point in the Alps, is also the highest mountain in Europe; it falls within the boundary line of France, and is 15,781 feet in height. Many lovely lakes fill up the Alpine valleys; of these, Geneva is the largest.

The Apennine chain, which is a spur of the Alps, runs through Central Italy from north to south, reaching into the heel of the boot, and down into the toe, and under the water, and out again into Sicily. These mountains are mostly covered with forests of chestnut trees, the nuts of which are a common food of the people. This range contains two volcanoes, or burning mountains, Vesuvius in Italy, and Etna in Sicily. These mountains do not always emit fire, but at times strange rumblings are heard from within them, and smoke and flame may be seen rising from an opening at the top called the *crater*. Then streams of melted matter, called lava, pour down the sides of the mountain, and showers of ashes are shot up into the air and fall upon the plain below. Many centuries ago, two towns which stood at the foot of Vesuvius were buried, the one under ashes, and the other under lava.

Mount Hecla, in Iceland, is also a volcano.

The Balkan Peninsula is full of mountains, the valleys between which are often only deep dark gorges. The Balkan range, which runs through the middle of the country from west to east, is sometimes called the back-bone of Turkey.

Spain is another mountainous peninsula. The Pyrenees Mountains separate it from France on the north, and several ranges cross the country from east to west. All the centre of Spain, that is, nearly half the peninsula, is a high table-land where green things are parched up in summer for want of rain.

Both the Carpathians and the various mountain ranges of Germany are rich in mineral treasures, and many men are employed in the mines. Gold and silver, quicksilver, copper, lead, and iron are found in these rich mountains.

LESSON VI.
RIVERS OF EUROPE.

THE map of Europe shows many river lines, for the whole continent is *well watered*.

The frozen plains of Northern Russia have, plainly, a northward slope, because the river Dwina flows in that direction into the White Sea. During the short, hot summer of these regions, Archangel, which stands at the mouth of the Dwina, is the great seaport of the north; but for more than half the year no ships can sail in those frost-bound seas.

Look, now, at the Scandinavian peninsula. The mountains which form the *waterparting* of the country run from north to south, so the land has an eastern and a western slope, down each of which the rivers. flow. As the mountains run close to the sea on the western side, the rivers have very short courses, and are, for the most part, mountain torrents hurrying to the ocean. The Swedish rivers have a rather longer slope to nm down, but as they only cross the country from the mountains to the Baltic Sea, where they empty themselves, none of these are large or important river.

The central plain of Europe, which lies along the southern coasts of the Baltic and North Seas, has a northward slope, for four or five large rivers empty themselves into these seas after a northward course. The Vistula and the Oder flow into the Baltic; the Elbe into the North Sea; and further west, the Rhine, coming out of Holland, enters this same sea. The Rhine is a wide, and, in its earlier course, a rapid river, which has its sources in the high Alps. It is more beautiful than any other river in Europe. Most of its course is in Germany, and the Germans love it well and sing songs in its praise.

The Seine, which is spanned by beautiful bridges and has the fair city of Paris on its banks, is another northward flowing river which empties itself into the English Channel.

Our own Thames, upon which London stands, flows down a slight eastward slope from the Cotswold Hills to the North Sea. Though much smaller than many of the rivers of the Continent, it is as famous as any for its great city, and for all the ships upon its waters. It has a wide mouth, into which the tide wave of the sea rushes. This kind of river mouth is called an *estuary*.

Now we come to the westward slope of the Continent, which we can easily discern, as half a dozen rivers in France and Spain flow in a westerly direction.

Flowing into the Bay of Biscay, is the Loire, a large French river which often overflows its banks, to the great distress of the people, whose houses and crops are thus destroyed.

Further south, the Gironda also opens into the Bay of Biscay. This is an estuary into which two French rivers flow.

The chief rivers of Spain, the Douro, Tagus, Guadiana, and Guadalquivir, flow down a westward slope towards the Atlantic, into which they empty themselves. Each of these rivers has its course between two of the mountain chains which cross the country.

The Ebro, another large Spanish river, enters the Mediterranean after a course down an eastward slope.

When we reach the southern shores of Europe, we expect the land to slope and the rivers to flow southward, as the land usually slopes towards the sea. This is the case with the Rhone, which rises among Alpine snows, flows through "Geneva's blue waters," makes a few turns upon entering France, and then flows southward with a wonderfully straight and rapid coarse to the Mediterranean, where it empties itself. Rising at so great a height, this river has a very rapid current; it tears up the ground in its hasty course, and brings with it much earth and stones, which it lays down at its mouth.

Land formed at the mouth of a river by the mud which it brings down is called a *delta*, from its resemblance to the Greek letter (Δ) so called; and most rivers divide, as the Rhone does, into several mouths when they reach the deltas they have formed.

The direction of the mountains which fill the two peninsulas of Italy and the Balkan prevents the rivers from having a southern course, wherefore we find that the Po and the Danube both flow down eastward slopes.

The Po, rising like the Rhone in the Alps, is also a very rapid river which flows across Northern Italy and into the Adriatic. As both the Po and its tributaries rise in high mountains, they tear along so fast that they bring much earth with them; so this river, also, has made a delta which stretches more than ten miles into the sea.

The wide and beautiful "blue Danube" flows into the Black Sea. You will see on the map that at one part of its course, near where it first forms the boundary between Roumania and Bulgaria, the mountains on either side of the river nearly meet. The narrowest part of this ravine is called the Iron Gate, where the river flows through a deep and narrow gorge more than a mile in length.

No mountains divert the courses of the slow rivers which flow through the flat steppes of Southern Russia; therefore these, the Dniester, the Dnieper, and the Don, creep down a slight southern slope to the Black Sea. So also does the Volga, which is the largest of all the rivers of Europe, and flows into the Caspian Sea. It is a slow, full river, which has never been near a mountain in all its coarse, and which never reaches the real sea; for the Caspian, though called a sea, is only a salt-water lake, as it does not open into the ocean.

QUESTIONS ON THE MAP OF EUROPE.

1. Name the empire which occupies the east of Europe.
2. What two northern countries form a peninsula?
3. What country is a small peninsula, pointing to the north?
4. What country is washed by the Bay of Biscay and the English Channel?
5. How many large peninsulas are there in the south of Europe?
6. What two countries form the most western of these?
7. Name the central peninsula. What small country lies to the north of it?
8. What two countries form the eastern peninsula?
9. Name the two great central countries?
10. What countries of Europe are washed by the Mediterranean? By the Bay of Biscay? By the North Sea? By the Baltic? By the Arctic Ocean?
11. Which are the mountainous countries of Europe?
12. What countries belong to the great plain partly or altogether?
13. What are the Swiss mountains called?
14. Name the mountains of Italy.
15. What mountains divide France from Spain?
16. What mountain-chain crosses Turkey from Asia on the east? On the South?
17. Where are the Scandinavian mountains?
18. What mountains divide Europe from Asia on the east? On the south?
19. Name three rivers that flow into the Baltic.
20. Three that enter the German Ocean.
21. The river on which Paris stands.
22. A river which flows into the Bay of Biscay.
23. The two largest rivers which flow through Spain and Portugal.
24. A French river which flows into the Mediterranean.
25. An Italian river which falls into the Adriatic.
26. A large river which enters the Black Sea from Turkey.
27. The two largest rivers which enter the Black Sea from Russia.
28. The large river which flows into the Caspian.
29. Through what countries does the Danube flow? The Rhine? The Rhone?
30. In what countries are the Po, the Thames, the Elbe, the Volga, the Seine, the Dou, the Loire?
31. What four seas open into each other on the south? How are they connected with each other and with the ocean?
32. Name the countries of Europe which are most broken into by the sea.
33. Name the largest islands in each of the seas of Europe. With what oceans are these seas connected?

LESSON VII.
THE BRITISH ISLES.

WHAT do we mean by the "British Isles"? The large island which contains the countries of England, Scotland, and Wales; and Ireland, the smaller island to the west. These are certainly *the* British Isles, in every way the most important of them; therefore the larger island is called *Great* Britain by way of distinction. But the two or three large and the numerous small islands off the coast of England, and the hundreds of islands off the Scotch coast, and the thousands of islets off the coast of Ireland, are also British isles. These are not *great* Britains by any means; some of them are very small indeed, being merely rocks, rising out of the sea, the wild haunts of swarms of sea-birds; others are large enough to be the homes of a few fisher folk; others, again, are large islands with farms and villages and busy towns upon them.

These British Isles keep on the whole close together, clustering round the large island of Great Britain; that, again, is only separated from the Continent by the narrow North Sea and the still narrower English Channel. If this narrow sea could be drained away we might go by rail to France and Holland and Belgium—a delightful idea to persons who wish to travel on the Continent, while they dread the miseries of sea-sickness.

So narrow are the Straits of Dover, which connect the English Channel with the North Sea, that a man might walk in a few hours the 21 miles which here divide England from France.

If the North Sea were to disappear, the slope to the bottom of its bed would be so slight that we should hardly know we were going down-hill. Imagine any of the low green hills of Southern England to be suddenly lifted from their bases, and set in the midst of this sea; they would not be covered, but would rise as islands, often high above the waters. Indeed, if the churches in your town could be taken up as they stand and placed on the sea floor, the spires would most likely rise above water; for the seas between Britain and the Continent are in few places more than 150 feet deep.

The fact is, that at one time, ages before "History" began, there were no British Isles and no North Sea, but the Continent stretched into the ocean a good way beyond the furthest coast of Ireland. Now, the eastern shores of England lie so low in some places that huge banks have been raised to keep out the sea; still lower do the opposite coasts of Holland and Belgium lie; wherefore these are called the Netherlands, or lowlands, while "Holland" merely means "hollow land." It is supposed that the land which once lay between these two opposite shores was also low, and that it sank at a slow rate, say a few inches in a year, until a sunken bed was formed. Then the waters of the Atlantic rushed in and filled the hollow, which thus became a narrow, shallow sea; and in this way the land we call Great Britain was cut off from the Continent and surrounded by water. In the same way, the ocean may have rushed into another hollow bed on the west, and so made another sea, cutting off the island which we call Ireland. And how are all the small islands which cluster round the great ones to be accounted for? Most likely these were at one time mountains, rising round the ancient shore; and when the sea covered the lowlands, the mountain tops remained above water, and now appear as islands.

Are you inclined to think it is a pity we should have been thus cut off from the Continent? It is, on the whole, a good thing for us; we Britons like to have our island home to ourselves, just as every English family likes to have a separate dwelling; while on the Continent it is usual for many families to live in a single large house. Being thus divided from them by the sea, we need never be disturbed by the disputes of other nations.

LESSON VIII
THE BRITISH ISLES.
PART II.

IT would be inconvenient for us, however, if we were cut off altogether from intercourse with foreign lands. British people are accustomed to make use of so many things which come from abroad that we should be badly off if the supply were stopped. For instance, what should we do without tea, coffee, and sugar, rice and treacle, or cotton to make our calico? Worse still, what should we do without *bread*? How sad it would be if there were not bread enough to be had for money to feed everybody in our swarming towns! You think, perhaps, it is only fruits and spices which will not flourish in our climate that we need to fetch from abroad, but that wheat and rye, oats and barley, grow freely in the British Isles. But the fact is, there are a great many more people in Britain, in England especially, than there is room to grow food for. If we were not a clever, industrious people, able to make things which other nations are glad to have instead of corn, we should be badly off.

But we make cotton stuffs and woollen stuffs, and every kind of article made of iron, besides many other useful things; and large countries, like parts of America and Russia, which have room to grow more corn than their people can eat, are glad enough to send us some of it in return for our manufactured goods, coal, and other things. Thus you see the British Isles depend a great deal upon this kind of exchange, which is called *commerce*. As Great Britain is an island, it can only trade with the rest of the world by means of ships; ships must carry out whatever British traders want to sell; ships must bring in such things as they wish to buy. Now, it is really a great deal easier and cheaper to fetch and carry on the sea than on land: the sea belongs to everybody, so it is free;

while, if there were no water-way, it would be necessary to pay some foreign ruler for leave to pass through his country. Again, no rails need be laid down, nor roads kept in order, for the ships to go upon. That breaking-in of the ocean which made Britain an island prepared the way for her to become a great nation; for the waters which divide her from all other lands are but highways for her ships. Then, the British seamen are hardy and brave, often brought up within sound of the sea, and come of forefathers who lived aboard ship; the blood of the hardy Norsemen—Saxons and Danes—runs in British veins.

There is perhaps no other country in the world quite so well placed for carrying on wide traffic on the seas. Fix a globe in such a position that one half will show nearly all the land in the world, the other half nearly all the water; the map on the opposite page shows you these hemispheres of land and water. Notice how Britain lies in the centre of the land hemisphere, with open sea-way to every country in the world that is not shut up in the middle of a continent. Across the narrow seas are various countries of Europe; to the west, across the broad Atlantic; lies America. A ship sailing south skirts the African coast. Bounding the point of Africa, she may either sail north to the countries of Southern Asia, or eastward to the great island of Australia.

It is a happy thing, also, that the seas round Britain are always open, and neither frost-bound, so that ships cannot enter them, nor made dangerous by floating icebergs. This is due partly to her *latitude*, her place in the north temperate zone; but no other lands which lie between 50° and 60° N. lat. have quite so pleasant a climate as Britain. One reason for this is that soft, moist winds blow from the south-west, across the ocean, and these winds make our winter days warmer, and our summer days cooler, than they would be if ours were an inland country. The influence of the warm Gulf

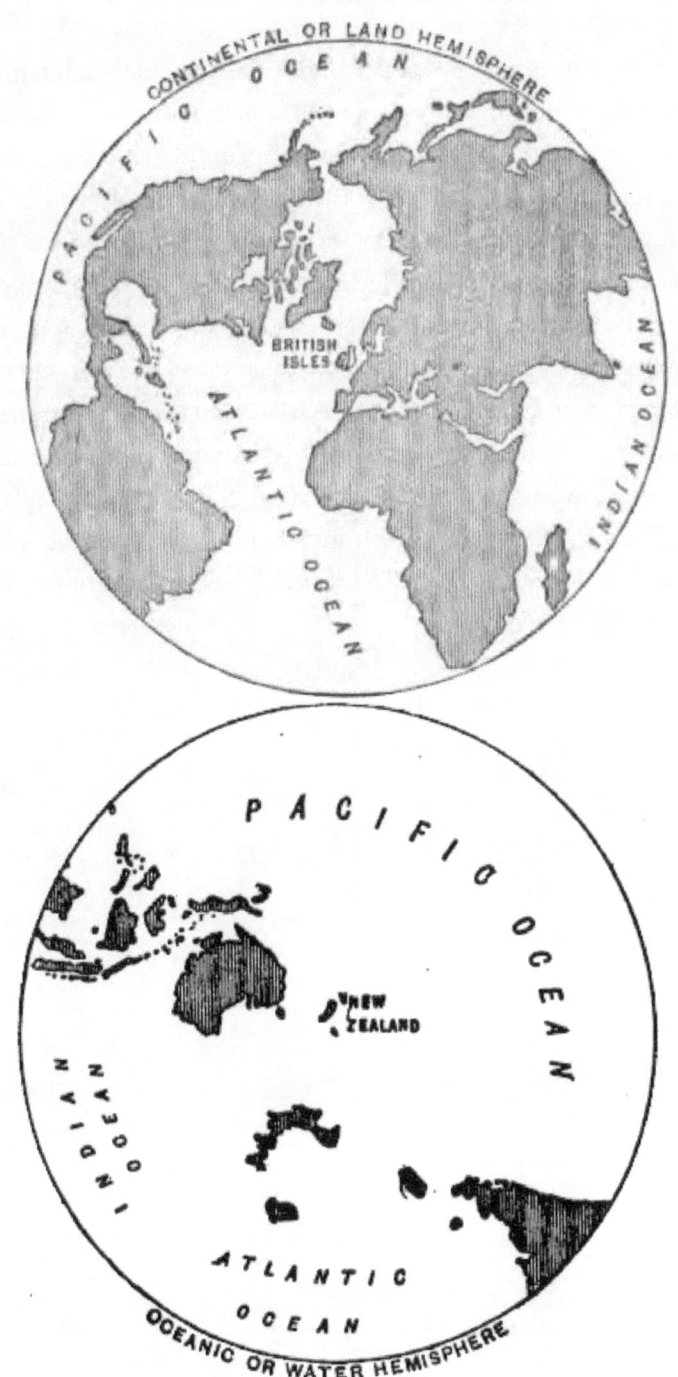

Stream is also, as we have seen, among the causes which temper the climate of Britain.

In point of size, the British Isles, important as they are, form only a very small part of the vast British Empire, upon which "the sun never sets." To begin in the east, and go round with the sun, our sovereign's dominions include the whole of Australia; the great country of India and two or three small possessions in Asia; the countries at the southern end of Africa, and some settlements on the West Coast; Gibraltar and some islands in the Mediterranean in Europe; all the northern lands of North America, and some small possessions in South America; the large islands of New Zealand in the Pacific, and several important islands in the Atlantic. Thus we see there are *British Possessions* in each of the Continents, and in every region of the globe.

LESSON IX.
THE CRUISE OF THE *SEAGULL*.

THE *Seagull* is a yacht, which, we propose, shall skim with white sail right round Great Britain; shall *circumnavigate* that island, in fact, with ourselves on board. In this way we shall make sure if the maps are right, and if Great Britain is an island indeed.

The first person we read of who made this coasting voyage was Julius Agricola, a great general who did much to subdue Britain for the Romans. It was all new to him; be went round the island that he might see the country, for he could not learn all about it from books of geography, as we may.

We shall start from Spithead, which is not a cape, as you might imagine, but is a broad, quiet harbour, where many ships may lie at anchor; it is the eastern half of the channel which divides the Isle of Wight from Hampshire; and so it is sheltered by the island from the rough sea-winds. We stop a little in this harbour, or *roadstead*, as it is called, to look at the beautiful green island, the "garden of England," where the white houses nestle among green trees, and spreading branches overarch the lanes. It is no wonder that Ryde and Cowes and the other pretty towns of the island are generally full of visitors.

Let us cross the water and enter Portsmouth Harbour, which is a large, still haven, with stately men-of-war lying at anchor. Portsmouth is what is called a *naval* port—that is to say, the ships of the navy come here to be repaired after stormy voyages, or after fighting some enemy on the open sea. Here too, war-ships are built, and here they are supplied with beef and bread, and blankets, and whatever else is needed for a long voyage.

Our "gull" shoots forward, past Selsea Bill, past the low, shingly Sussex coast, where there are three or four warm, pleasant, bathing-places, of which Brighton is the gayest and most fashionable. Crowds of fishing-smacks swarm about us, all out for the mackerel fishing. They will be out all night, and early in the morning boatloads of beautifully marked, shining fish will be emptied for sale upon the beaches of the fishing towns.

That great, white headland stretching out before us is Beachy Head, whose cliffs of white chalk rise 600 feet from the sea.

After passing a bit of low shore, we come again upon white cliff's—

"The white chalk cliffs of Dover."

That is Dover Castle upon the cliff, and yonder is a passenger-boat crossing to Calais, for we are in the Strait of Dover.

Rounding the point called the South Foreland—*Fore*-land, because it comes forward, comes to the fore—we are careful to keep close to shore, and find ourselves in strangely still water. We are in the *Downs*, which is another roadstead or harbour. But what shuts it in? We see land on the left, but nothing save open sea on the right. There is land on this side also, though we cannot see it;—a high sandbank ten miles long rises nearly to the surface of the water, and shuts in these *roads* for the ships. These Goodwin Sands form a friendly haven for vessels within the Downs; but outside, the mariners dread the treacherous banks, for many a good ship has struck upon them.

We pass the North Foreland, and turn towards a great opening on our left. There are busy towns on the shores, and much shipping is around us; and the further we go up this opening, the more do we seem to be sailing through a forest of masts. We are going up with the tide, and at the same time a river is forcing itself down to the sea. We are in the broad estuary of the Thames, the chief of English rivers. The ships have all come to bring merchandise to

London, the greatest city and the greatest port in the world; or to carry away the goods which the London merchants send all over the globe. There are large docks—quiet pools, walled round—built on each side of the river to hold the ships.

LESSON X.
THE CRUISE OF THE *SEAGULL*.
PART II.

WE sail out of the Thames, and northward, past the low, flat shores of the eastern counties. Again, we find ourselves amongst a host of brown-sailed fishing-smacks. We are in a herring fishery this time—the great Yarmouth fishery, and the silvery herring will be carried into this pleasant seaport-town, to be salted and dried and made into "Yarmouth bloaters."

Rounding the eastern shoulder of England, we find ourselves in the Wash, and into this opening four slow, dull rivers empty themselves—the Witham, the Welland, the Nen, and the Great Ouse. The Fens lie all round the Wash, and stretch far inland. These Fens are quite the lowest part of the eastern counties, and lie so very low that in some places the sea is only kept out by means of embankments and sea walls.

To look at it on the map, one would think the Wash would be a capital place for ships, but it is full of shifting sandbanks, and is not at all safe.

The Humber, the next large opening we enter, is also full of these dangerous sandbanks. It is the estuary of two rivers—the Trent, the great middle river of England, and the Ouse, which flows through Yorkshire. Upon its northern shore stands the large seaport town of Hull. A glance at the map of Europe will enable us to judge with what countries Hull trades. Across the North Sea, and through the narrow channels which lead into the Baltic, do her ships go, and from the countries round the Baltic they bring corn, timber, flax, tallow, and hides.

No cape upon the east coast stands out to sea so boldly as Flamborough Head. A lighthouse rises from its cliffs of white chalk; and upon these cliffs in ages long gone by the Danes kept up huge bonfires to light their black ships over the stormy sea. Thus this cape came by its name, the headland of the *flame*.

As we sail northwards we pass the mouths of the Tees, the Wear, and the Tyne, all full of shipping, because there are busy seaport towns upon each of these three rivers. The chief of these ports is Newcastle on the Tyne. "Coal to Newcastle" people say when you give them more of what they have too much of already. He would be indeed a foolish merchant who sent coal to Newcastle; for it stands upon a wide coalfield, and sends out thousands of vessels every year, which carry Newcastle coal to London, to France, to the Baltic, and to the countries round the Mediterranean.

Passing many *colliers*, we sail by the little Farn Islands, upon one of which Grace Darling lived, and by Holy Island, the home of holy men in days when much of Britain was pagan. You are wondering, perhaps, who Grace Darling was. She was a brave girl, whose father took care of the lighthouse on Farn Island, and who saved some shipwrecked mariners in a terrible storm at great risk of her own life. At last we come in sight of Berwick, the border town where England and Scotland meet.

And now we have sailed up the whole of the eastern side of England. We have seen some dreary-looking sandy wastes here and there. We have passed a few busy seaports and some pleasant-looking bathing-places. But nearly everywhere, at a little distance from the shore, we have seen farm lands—green meadows or pasture-fields, with cattle feeding in them; corn-fields, or turnip or cloverfields. Farming is the chief work carried on in the eastern counties; and the land lies so low nearly all along the coast that from the deck of our boat we are able to see a good way inland. We catch sight of many snug farm-houses in pleasant spots; and we see the labourers abroad in the fields, and the scattered villages where these farm-labourers live.

LESSON XI.
ROUND NORTH BRITAIN.

"N.B." people usually put on letters addressed to Edinburgh or Glasgow; and in this case " N .B:" means, not *Nota Bene*—"Take Notice"—but "North Britain." Scotland is North Britain, and South Britain consists of England and Wales.

We still make steadily northwards, keeping as close to the shore as we can, in order to see if there is anything to mark the fact that

BASS ROCK, FIRTH OF FORTH

we have left England behind and are coasting Scotland. Long ranges of rather bare rounded hills, with sheep feeding on the short turf upon their slopes, stretch nearly to the coast. One range, the Lammermuir Hills, ends in St. Abb's Head. What is that curious mass of rock rising like a sugar-loaf steep out of the sea? That is the Bass Rock, 400 feet high, and so steep that only on one side is it possible to land upon it. And now we are in the broad, beautiful Firth of

Forth. This name shows we are in another country; there are no *firths* in England, but you will find many on the map of Scotland. Firth (fiord) is the old Norse name for an estuary or opening; and the Firth of Forth is the estuary of the river Forth.

A sail up the Forth is full of interest; there are pleasure-boats and fishing-smacks and a few merchantmen upon the waters, but not many of these last, for there are no good harbours in the Forth. Even Leith, the seaport of Edinburgh, cannot give comfortable quarters to the ships that ply her trade. We pass busy towns on either shore, and pleasant bathing-places, standing among trees and gardens; and we see the fisher-wives come down to the boats to get their stock of "caller herrin'" (fresh herring). In what a curious way they carry their fish! Those huge, deep baskets on their backs, supported by means of a leathern strap passed round their foreheads, are quite new to us.

We must land to see the beautiful city of Edinburgh, the capital of Scotland. The old town and the new town are built upon two opposite hills, facing each other, and the valley between them is laid out in pleasant gardens.

The tall, quaint old houses of the old town—eight or nine stories high sometimes—rise on the steep hill-side, street above street, in the strangest way. And at one end of this hill is the castle of Edinburgh, which looks so like the great rocks on which it is built that you might take it for part of the mountain pile.

At the other end of the old town is the beautiful palace of Holyrood, the home of the Scottish kings when Scotland had its own sovereign: and not only to ancient Holyrood, but to half the houses in the old streets, strange tales of other days belong.

Edinburgh is not a busy trading or manufacturing town like London; it is quite small in comparison; and perhaps the printing and publishing of books is the chief trade carried on there.

Sailing out of the Forth, and up the North Sea, we are warned that there is danger ahead by the lighthouse which stands opposite to the mouth of the Tay. As it is high water, this lighthouse seems to rise sheer out of the sea; but we know it must be built upon the Bell Rock, that famous Inchcape Rock to which belongs the story of the Abbot of Aberbrothok and his bell.

We have not time to go up the silver Tay, not even to see the seaport town of "bonnie Dundee."

Continuing northwards, we pass a rock-bound coast with huge caverns in the cliffs in which are swarms of sea-birds; and we row into one of these caverns with lighted torches, to the terror of the birds, which flap about us and scream in an alarming way. The Bullers of Buchan are famous arched rocks upon this coast.

Before reaching Buchan-Ness, we should have stopped on our way to see Aberdeen, a seaport town at the mouth of the Dee, as its name might tell us, for *Aber* means river mouth. We may see ships being laden at its wharves with a heavy freight—pillars, slabs, fountains, and other objects made of polished granite. There are granite quarries near the town; and much of this beautiful stone is brought here from the Cairngorm mountains also, to be polished in the famous granite works of Aberdeen. Rounding the great eastern shoulder, a straighter shoulder than that of England, we go by a low straight coast towards the Moray Firth. If we enter this Firth, we may sail right through Scotland by the Caledonian Canal, which cuts the country in two; but we have yet much to see before we make for the west.

Northward still, up to Duncansby Head and across the boisterous Pentland Firth, we go, for we are bound for the Orkneys. How our little boat is tossed about in this stormy channel, and how thankful we are to near land! There is not much to repay us for our rough voyage. We land upon Pomona, the largest of the islands, and from there cruise about among the dozen or so of larger islands which are inhabited. There are over sixty of these Orkney Isles altogether, but of them, some forty barren and desolate islets are left altogether to the sea-fowl and rabbits. Those which are inhabited are dreary enough, consisting of little but wide heather wastes, huge boulders, sandhills full of rabbit warrens, swamps, and lakes. Occasionally, in a sheltered spot, a patch of corn is to be seen; and there are many fishing villages on the shores. The people live upon fish, and trade with fish, and very fishy their villages smell. Cod-fish, lobsters, and herrings are sent hence to the London markets.

A sail across a channel nearly fifty miles wide brings us to another group of which we know something beforehand. We are familiar with the shaggy little Shetland ponies; and every one has seen the fine, beautiful knitting of the Shetland women, in veils and shawls and other woollen garments. Is it our fancy, or are these islands really more rainy and misty and desolate, more swampy and rocky than the Orkneys? Again we see rabbits disappearing in the sandhills; the islands swarm with them, and the Shetlanders make a good deal by selling their skins. These are a larger group of islands than the Orkneys, and as many as forty are inhabited. Mainland is the largest.

LESSON XII.
THE OCEAN SHORES.

Look at the map and you will see that the *Ocean* shore is the western shore, for much of Western Scotland is washed, not by some narrow sea, but by the broad Atlantic itself. Did you ever see such a ragged and broken coast, bordered by a perfect fringe of islands. There is one other country on the map of Europe with such another jagged edge—Norway, further to the north; and the shores of Norway, also, are ocean-washed.

Western Scotland is full of mountain ranges which end close to the shore, and between these ranges are long valleys, up which the ocean rushes, filling them, and thus we have the long deep "lochs" which cut up this coast.

Let us round Cape Wrath and sail down the western coast to explore some of these lochs. We need not enter more than two or three, for they are all much alike—narrow mountain glens with a floor of sea. We are impressed by the stillness and strangeness of the scene, the awful height of the cliffs, and the clear depths of the loch, which reflects every bush, almost every blade of grass. Yet there are sounds in the stillness—the endless calls of the sea-birds and the roar of the waves beyond the loch. Signs of life there are,

A LOCH

too. Those white dots as big as mushrooms are sheep which have straggled high up the cliffs in search of the scanty herbage they yield. See! there is one now making for "fresh fields and pastures new." These mountain sheep become as nimble and sure-footed as goats. In another loch, not even a leaping goat disturbs the stillness; so sheer and steep do its mountain walls rise from the sea that there is no foothold for the surest-footed creature.

How is it that, being on the Atlantic, we do not see the sun set in the sea, but behind mountainous land which lies to the west? Those are the heights of the Hebrides, the Western Isles, several of which stretch in a long row that is sometimes called Long Island.

We are in the channel called the "Minch," and may either sail across to those *Outer* Hebrides, of which Lewis is the largest, or we may keep close to the mainland and explore Skye, the largest of the *Inner* Hebrides. These islands are not like the rather flat and dreary groups to the north-east. Many of them, Skye especially, are wild and beautiful, with mountains, waterfalls, and lakes; and many summer visitors come to fish in the lochs or to shoot over the moors.

The islanders are busy enough, both in summer and winter; they fish, rear large herds of black cattle, and, in every house, they make enough cloth for their own clothes, and tables and benches for their use.

We must visit Iona, the Holy Island of Scotland, a bare little isle, where good missionaries lived and taught in days when Scotland was a pagan land.

Staffa, too, we must see, for the sake of its famous cavern, which looks as if cunning workmen had built its walls of countless regular columns of polished stone. It is about seventy yards long, and is one of the most remarkable caverns in the world.

We are anxious to get into the Firth of Clyde, and as there is a shorter way, we shall not round the curious long tongue of land called the Mull of Cantyre. We must be content to miss Jura, and Islay, the "Queen of the Hebrides." A canal has been cut across the top of the long "Mull," through which we go, and soon find ourselves in the lovely Firth of Clyde. It is a broad, beautiful estuary, with islands rising out of it; its banks are high and wooded; and handsome houses, and pleasant bright watering-places stand among the trees. As we sail up the river we leave trees and pleasure places behind and find ourselves between long lines of building yards, where there are vessels in every stage of progress. Higher still, and we are among wharves full of sea-going ships, and presently we arrive at the large and busy seaport of Glasgow, the busiest town in Scotland.

Sailing down the narrow North Channel which divides Scotland from Ireland, we come out so close to the Isle of Man that we may as well run across. It is 30 miles long, and has two or three pleasant bathing-places on its shores. There is a range of hills in the middle of the island. The people are called Manx, and had formerly a strange language of their own. The herring fishery occupies many of the inhabitants, and others work in the lead mines and slate quarries of the island. One odd thing that everybody knows about the Isle of Man is that the Manx cats have no tails.

We have not time to explore the north-west coast of England, nor even to see the red headland of St. Bees. We make direct for Liverpool, the great seaport of the west, and one of the most famous in the world. What crowds of ships there are in its long line of docks!—ships from every part of the world. Many of these have come from America with cargoes of cotton, for Liverpool is the port to which all the raw cotton is brought for our great Lancashire manufacture.

LESSON XIII.
THE PRINCIPALITY.

WALES is "the Principality" now, because the eldest son of the English sovereign is Prince of Wales. At one time Wales had a prince of its own who spoke the native Welsh language. But these wild Welsh princes and their wilder people were troublesome neighbours to the English. They were constantly breaking over the border, and carrying off crops and cattle.

To put an end to this state of things the English king, Edward I., came with an army, conquered Wales, and had the last of the Welsh princes put to death at Shrewsbury. Most likely you know what followed; how the Welsh were so sad to lose their chief that the king promised them another native prince who could not speak a word of English, and brought out his own little baby son, born in Carnarvon Castle, at least so the story goes.

English is spoken in some of the towns now, but the country people understand only their native tongue. Follow a group of market-women as they trot along the road, knitting in hand and chattering fast in Welsh, and you feel you are really in a foreign country; and quite foreign these women look in their tall beaver hats, something like the tall hats worn by men in England, and their handsome cloaks.

The word "Wales" means "foreign," land of the foreigners. This name was given to the country by the Saxons who conquered England, because they looked on the people of Wales as foreigners. But, in fact, the Welsh should have been a great deal more at home in England than these Saxon conquerors, for they were the old British people to whom all Britain once belonged. They were driven westward to take shelter in this mountain land by these strangers from over the sea; and there they have remained ever since.

To turn them out of Wales was too hard a task for any English king; for the country is full of mountains and ravines and wild hiding-places, where the natives were safe, because no English army could find them out.

Now, however, Wales is quite a part of England, and numbers of English people go every year to spy out these secret biding-places. For many parts of this mountain country are exceedingly beautiful, and there is no pleasanter way of spending a summer holiday than in exploring the lovely valleys and majestic mountains of North Wales.

Tourists generally enter Wales by way of the city of Chester; we may follow the Dee valley as far as the lovely Vale of Llangollen, or we may go by the north coast, where there is much to be seen. First, we stop at Holywell, a rather large and busy town, to see the well of Saint Winifred. This is a wonderful spring which is always pouring out an immense stream of water; and for centuries it was believed that whoever drank of this water would be cured of whatever disease he had. Saint Winifred was a holy maiden whose head was struck off by a cruel knight; and where the head fell, says the legend, this beautiful spring gushed out; wherefore it was a *holy* well with power to work miraculous cures. But people are too wise nowadays to believe these pretty legends.

We walk out upon Great Orme's Head and are nearly blown away by the strong wind; and we go over the old castle of Conway; and then go on to Bangor, to see the huge Penrhyn slate quarries, in which hundreds of men swarm like so many ants. From Bangor, we cross the Menai Bridge, a wonderful suspension bridge hung so high above the Menai Straits that the largest ships can pass full-sail underneath. Or we may get by rail into the island of Anglesea, across the famous Britannia Bridge. It was found necessary to make this railway bridge, which is more than a quarter of a mile long, because many persons go from Chester to Anglesea, in order to take the Dublin packet from Holyhead. These used to be ferried ever to the island; but in stormy weather no boat could cross the strait, and the passengers ran the risk of missing the steamboat which should take them to Ireland. We see the copper-mines of Anglesea, and return by one of the bridges, for we wish to get to Carnarvon, that we may go over the castle where the first English Prince of Wales was born.

And now we are near one of the great sights of North Wales, the mighty Snowdon, the monarch of British mountains; or, at any rate, the highest south of the Clyde (3590 feet). There he stands, with his three great summits of nearly equal height, surrounded by other lofty mountains, as a king by his noble courtiers. Indeed, nearly the whole of Wales is full of mountains: towering heights, and deep glens, and lovely vales, and waterfalls, meet us everywhere.

Going almost due south from Snowdon, through the beautiful mountainous county of Merioneth, we reach Cader Idris, another of the giants of the land. And, further south, almost in a line with the other two, is the huge mass of Plynlimmon, which, like Snowdon, has three summits. We must climb this mountain and search in its bosom for the source of the Severn, the queen of our English rivers.

A good deal of Central Wales, though mountainous, is not beautiful: it is a dreary waste of craggy height and moor and marsh. And the black mountains of South Wales receive their name from the dark and gloomy appearance they present—especially when the heather is not in bloom.

There is a very large coalfield in South Wales, and at Swansea there are great smelting works to which the copper ore of Cornwall is sent to be *smelted*, that is, to have the copper melted, and so separated from the earth it is mixed with. We have not had time to visit Dolgelly and Welshpool and the other flannel-making towns of North Wales. Nor can we see St. David's Head, nor Milford Haven, the fine harbour in Pembrokeshire.

LESSON XIV.
THE WESTERN HORN.

Just because the coast of this strangely shaped horn is the most beautiful and interesting part of our English seaboard, we must not linger now to explore it. This western horn begins at the mouth of the Severn and stretches westward to the Land's End, pushing boldly forth into the stormy ocean, and nearly every mile of the way has some beauty or interest.

We start from Bristol, the second great seaport of the west, in whose harbour are crowded ships from the south and east, ships from the warm countries round the Mediterranean, and ships from Ireland; and these have brought in stores of good things, dried fruits and wine; butter and bacon. On we go, past the lovely cliff-coasts of North Devon, where shrubs and flowering plants grow down to the water's edge. The towns and villages are perched upon the high cliffs, or nestle in snug green valleys with rocky walls. The Cornish coast is more rugged than that of Devon, but nothing can be more beautiful than the little *porths*, or inlets where the broken cliffs let in the sea.

As we sail towards the Land's End, we can see the Cornish heights swelling, rugged and bare, all through the middle of the peninsula. Barren as they look, we know that these bills and moors are really rich; that thousands of miners are constantly at work, digging out the veins of tin and copper ore which run under this rough crust.

How the people are swarming upon the beach! and what are those boats about? We are below the town of St. Ives, and the pilchards are coming; we can see the great shoal darkening the waters in the distance. The fishers are letting out the huge *seine* net, with which they catch millions in a single taking. And now

LANDS END.

we are at the Land's End itself—a good name for this lofty granite table, round which the furious ocean dashes and roars! *Land's End* indeed, for between it and far distant America is nothing but the wide Atlantic waters.

Past Mount's Bay, and round to the Lizard we go; and here we must see the caves, the Parlour and the Drawing-room, whose walls are of a beautiful striped rock of various colours.

We pass the Eddystone, and wonder how it was possible to build a lighthouse so far out to sea. As a storm is rising, we make for Plymouth Sound; for once within the *Breakwater*, we know we are safe. This huge stone wall, rising from the sea-bottom, keeps out the breakers, and the waters within the Sound are still as a lake. Plymouth is a busy town, being a large *naval* port to which the ships of the navy come and go. There is a famous dockyard here where these ships are built or repaired and supplied with everything necessary for a long voyage.

We must not stop to look at the beautiful *combes* of South Devon; these are valleys between hill ranges, where the villages nestle amongst apple orchards. Nor can we go up the Exe, to see the city of Exeter, the "Queen of the West." As we pass the Dorset coast, we notice Portland Point, a curious long narrow tongue of land which stretches far into the sea. Presently, we are once more in Spithead, the spot we started from; and we *know* that Great Britain is an island, because we have sailed round it.

LESSON XV.
FROM JOHN O'GROAT'S TO LAND'S END.

JOHN O'GROAT built himself a house on the beach near Duncansby Head. From that point to Land's End is the greatest length of Great Britain, 600 miles; a distance which it would take a man five weeks to walk at the rate of twenty miles a day.

The first part of the journey, as far as Glenmore, is through the Highlands. Look at the map, and you will see how few towns are marked in this district, and how many mountains, rivers, and lakes. It is a huge, high tableland, a heather waste, with bogs and granite boulders; where high, solitary mountains rise, rugged and bare, above the rest, such as Ben More, Ben Wyvis, Ben Attow, all over 8000 feet. "Ben" is the Gaelic word for mountain. This rugged land is thinly inhabited by a Gaelic people, and the few Highlanders we meet wear the short petticoat, or kilt, speak only in Gaelic, and, if they are musical, play upon the bagpipes.

What are their occupations? Many of them look after the mountain sheep and herds of black cattle you may see trying to gather a scanty living in these craggy pastures. This district is far too mountainous and barren to be cultivated, and, indeed, hardly yields food for the cattle; so these and the sheep are brought in due time to various fairs by the Highland drovers, aided by their clever dogs. There they are bought by Lowland farmers, and are driven either to the Scotch Lowlands or to rich English pastures to be fattened for the market. The *trysts* of Falkirk are the most famous of these cattle fairs.

The Highlanders have another occupation. Every autumn brings many strangers to these high moorlands, who come to "stalk" the red deer, to shoot grouse, or to fish for salmon or trout in the lakes and streams; and to these gentlemen many of the natives hire themselves out as guides and servants.

Glenmore, the long, narrow valley or "dip" which goes across the country from Loch Linnhe to the Moray Firth, has at the bottom of it a line of lakes, long and narrow like itself. These have been joined together by cuttings made to bold water; so that a long waterway, which is called the Caledonian Canal, passes right through Scotland. Glenmore, with its lakes, is only an example of the countless long narrow glens with long narrow lakes which cut up the whole of these northern Highlands.

To the south of Glenmore the ground rises again, and we are once more in the Highlands. Here, a wide-spreading mountain chain, 100 miles long; runs across the country. This is the Grampian range, which has the highest mountains, not only in Scotland, but in Great Britain, namely, Ben Nevis and Ben Macdhui, both over 4000 feet high; and great hoary giants they are, which wear a snow cap half the year, and bury their heads in the clouds.

Ben Ledi and Ben Lomond are not so high, but they attract more visitors; for these mountains rise where the barren highlands border on the green and fertile lowlands. Where this is the case the country is exceedingly beautiful; and many visitors come yearly to see the Trosachs—a wooded ravine and mountain pass which opens out upon lovely lakes with towering mountains round them. There is Loch Katrine, with "fair Ellen's isle," and, further on, Loch Lomond, the largest lake in Britain, with wooded islands upon its bosom. Now we enter the Lowlands—the broad valleys of the Forth and Clyde; this is a green and pleasant country, and only low as compared with the Highlands we have just left. From the rather steep bill on which Stirling Castle stands we have a delightful view of the plains, where we see green pasture-fields, wide farms, and sparkling streams. The "Links of Forth" are the most curious sight; the river doubles and turns again and again in its green valley, so that it looks like the links of a chain. This part of Scotland is a great farming district; perhaps nowhere in the world is land better farmed than here, especially in the eastern counties, where potatoes are grown in great quantities for the London market. The Scots themselves prefer oatmeal porridge and oat-cake, and oats are the principal corn crop.

In this part of Scotland, too, lie the coal-fields, and here are the manufacturing towns: Paisley and Renfrew, famous for shawls and woollen goods; Carron, near Falkirk, and Airdrie, for ironworks; Glasgow, for cotton, woollen, and other manufactures; Dundee and Dunfermline, further north, for linen; Stirling and Galashiels, for Scotch tweed, and shawls.

Southern Scotland is another "Highlands," though less lofty and ragged than the northern. It is crossed by several ranges of hills—the Cheviots, which divide Scotland from England, the Lowthers, the Ochils, and others. These ranges are all very much alike, consisting of smooth, grassy hills, without any particular beauty, whereon many sheep are fed. The river valleys or "dales" between these are, however, often very beautiful.

The Lowland Scotch are like the English in every way; they speak the same language and have much the same national character, because, like the English, they are descended from Saxon tribes who settled north as well as south of the Tweed. These drove the ancient people of Scotland to take refuge among the northern mountains, just as the Saxons who took England drove the Britons into Wales. For this reason the Highlanders still speak the old Gaelic tongue, and are a distinct people in their customs and dress, as well as in their language.

For nearly three centuries Scotland has been under the rule of the same king or queen as England, because it so happened that when the English Queen Elizabeth died, the King of Scotland was her nearest relative, and was therefore the next heir to the English throne. Before that time, when Scotland had a king of its own, the two countries were seldom at peace. The land on each side of the Cheviots was called "the Border," and the Scotch and English "Borderers" made continual war upon one another.

LESSON XVI.
FROM JOHN O'GROATS TO LAND'S END.
PART II.

HAVING crossed the Cheviots, we may now try to get a "bird's-eye view" of England. The great moorland ridge, called the Pennine chain, which runs through Northern England as far as Derbyshire, divides the three northern counties on the east from the three on the west. These moors are wild heather wastes, over which it is not easy to tramp; and there are deep ravines among the rocks, and huge crags and boulders scattered about, and wide morasses, like sponges filled with water, into which one might easily sink. From these do the bonny rivers which flow down the slope on either side gather their waters. No river *crosses* the moors, because the Pennine chain is the *waterparting* of Northern England, that is, it divides the rivers which flow down one slope from those which flow down the other.

Close under the hills, and stretching from Leeds to Nottingham, is a wide coal-field, and upon this coal-field are built many busy towns engaged in a great manufacture for which coal is needed. These are the clothing towns, Leeds, Bradford, Halifax, Huddersfield, and others, where wool is spun and woven into cloths and stuffs; and the wool is cleansed in the pretty rivers, whose waters are further blackened with dye-stuffs.

Sheffield is another busy town upon the Yorkshire coal-field; it is famous all over the world for its knives and other edge-tools. On the Lancashire side of the hills there is another coal-field; and upon this, also, are some of the largest and busiest towns in England, which bristle all over with tall mill-chimneys.

This district is the seat of the great cotton manufacture, of which Manchester, the largest town in England after London, is the centre. Preston, Bolton, Blackburn, Bury, Wigan, and other towns are engaged in making the cotton cloths which English ships carry all over the world.

On the eastern side, the moors slope down to the broad valley of the Ouse, which is called the Vale of York; it is well covered with cornfields and pasture-fields, farms and villages, and is the largest valley in England. The ancient city of York, which contains the most stately and beautiful cathedral in the country, stands upon the Ouse.

The Pennine Mountains are grand and rugged, but they are less famous for their beauty than are the Cumbrian Group, which fill much of the counties of Cumberland and Westmorland with rugged *fells* and towering peaks. Three of these, Helvellyn, Skiddaw, and Scafell, are over 3000 feet in height, and are the highest mountains in England. These mountains do not run in a line, but are gathered together, one great ridge swelling up behind another; and between the ridges are lovely valleys, and at the bottom of many of the valleys lie still, blue lakes.

We must not linger in this beautiful *Lake District*; nor must we stop at the *Peak*, the name which is given to the rugged and beautiful mountain country in which the moors of the Pennine chain end. Past the silk-mills of Derby town and over the Trent river, we hasten onwards to Bardon Hill, in Leicestershire. It is quite a low hill, which does not rise much higher from the ground than a church steeple; but it is well worth climbing, because from its summit about a quarter of England may be seen. This must be a very flat part of the country, you will say, to be seen from so low a hill. It is true; the middle of England is a wide plain, though we must not picture it to ourselves as perfectly flat; pleasant uplands with clumps of trees rise everywhere excepting in the east. There, round the Wash, and stretching far inland, are the low fenlands,

COAL MINE.

from which the river waters can hardly be carried away, and the sea can hardly be kept out.

But we shall see all this from our hill. To the west of us the view is cut off by a thick smoke-cloud. This cloud hangs over the "Black Country," so called because a great industry is carried on there which blackens trees, and buildings, and the very air. South Staffordshire and North Warwickshire lie under this smoke-cloud; below the surface there is a wide coal-field, where many *pitmen* labour; and, above ground, there are many blast-furnaces belching out smoke and flame, and large furnaces lit up by the glare of red-hot metal, and noisy with the clang of many hammers. These are the great ironworks of England, where machines and tools, bedsteads, grates, gates, and all kinds of iron articles are manufactured. Iron lies under the surface here along with the coal which is necessary to work it. Most of the labouring men are workers in iron; and the towns, Wolverhampton, Bilston, Dudley, and some others, produce iron goods. Birmingham is the largest and most famous of these towns; it is a place where many curious and useful manufactures are carried on—pins, pens, buttons, bolts, and other things small and great, from a screw to a huge engine, are made here.

We can discern another smoke-cloud to the north of this; it must lie over North Staffordshire, where, we know, are the Potteries. Most of the earthenware used in England, as well as a great deal which is sent abroad, is manufactured in Burslem, Stoke, and the long line of towns and villages connected with them. The Potteries stand upon another coal-field, great fires being required to bake the potter's ware.

LESSON XVII.
FROM JOHN O'GROAT'S TO LAND'S END.
PART III.

IF it were not for this smoke-cloud, we might get a glimpse of the flat Cheshire plain, where we should see green pastures everywhere, with many cows at grass, from whose milk the famous Cheshire cheese is made. Under part of Cheshire lies, not coal, as in the adjoining county, but a wide field of salt, which miners are employed to dig from the earth.

What is that green dip we notice in the land, which, as it bends to the north, becomes a wide valley, with gleaming water at the bottom? That is the valley of the Trent, the great river of middle England, on its way to the mouth of the Humber. We may distinguish the towers of Nottingham Castle, which stands upon the Trent; and a little to the northeast, away from the river, we can discern the more distant towers belonging to the beautiful cathedral of Lincoln, which stands upon a hill; from this hill we might overlook a great deal of the flat, farming county of Lincolnshire. Many chimneys, you will notice, rise to the north of us, in the direction of the county of Nottingham, as well as in Leicestershire itself. These are the chimneys of the "mills" where stockings and lace are made. Nottingham and Leicester are both busy manufacturing towns.

As we turn to the east and the south we may bid farewell to mill-chimneys and smoke. The manufactures and mines belong to the north and west of England; the eastern and south-eastern counties are all laid out in wide farms. Yellow fields and green fields with many cattle meet the eye everywhere; there are fields of wheat and barley, of clover and grass, of potatoes, turnips, and beans—food for men and food for cattle; for to produce food seems to be the business of these pleasant farming counties.

We cannot see far to the south-west, because hills break the view. Let us go across country to the Cotswold Hills in Gloucestershire, and from these we shall be able to see the beautiful valley of the Severn, the great river of the west. This is a very pretty part of England; the four counties in the Severn valley are hilly and woody, and are full of apple and pear orchards; cider and perry are made from the fruit. Famous cheese is made in Gloucestershire, which is what is called a dairy county, that is, many cows are kept there for the sake of their milk, which is made into butter or cheese. A good many mill-chimneys may be counted in Gloucestershire, and in the two counties to the south of it, for the well-known west-country *broadcloth*, is made in Stroud, Frome, Bradford, and a few other places.

The Thames, the most famous of all British rivers, rises in these Cotswold Hills. We cannot choose a better spot from which to see its valley than the towers of Windsor Castle, the Queen's palace. The Castle is built upon a "princely brow" overhanging the river, and from the Keep the greater part of thirteen counties may be seen. These are, for the most part, pleasant counties, green and woody, with fertile fields, farms, and villages; and they contain many of the beautiful dwellings of the nobility.

As we have already spoken of the strangely shaped peninsula which ends in the Land's End, we have only now to see the "chalk" counties. All the south-eastern shires, from Wilts to Kent, are composed, for the most part, of chalk; dig below the surface soil anywhere, and white chalk is the rock you come to. This chalk country begins with Salisbury Plain in Wiltshire, and from there three or four long ranges of low rounded chalk hills branch out. The most important of these are the North and South Downs, in Surrey and Sussex, upon which many sheep are fed, for the hills are covered with rich green turf, delightful to walk upon and very good to eat, at least, so the sheep would consider. These southeastern counties are among the farming shires. Kent is famous for its great cherry-orchards and its hop grounds.

LESSON XVIII.
FROM JOHN O'GROAT'S TO LAND'S END.
PART IV.

WE who live in this pleasant and peaceable land do not think it strange that farmers should live in lonely country houses where there are neither policemen nor soldiers to take care of them, and yet should drive their cattle afield, and raise their crops, as if they had no fear. But it is a thing to be proud of and thankful for that England is governed by wise laws well carried out; and this is why English people, whether in town or country, have not often cause to be uneasy about the safety of their property. These laws by which England is governed have been hundreds of years in making, yet new ones are added from year to year, as they are wanted.

The gentlemen who help to make the laws are called Members of Parliament. Every large town and every county chooses two or more "Members" to send up to the great Parliament Houses at Westminster. These meet to talk matters over in one hall or "House," called the House of Commons. All the great noblemen in the land meet in another hall in the same building, which is called the House of Lords. Before any new law comes into force the greater part of the "Commons" must agree to it, and the greater part of the "Lords," and, last of all, the Queen must give her consent. Of course this leads to a great deal of talking, and the word "Parliament" means "talking"; the Houses of Parliament are the Talking Houses. Thus Great Britain is governed not by the Sovereign alone, but by the Sovereign, the Lords, and the Commons, who are all concerned in the making of laws.

We must now say something of the English people, to whom this pleasant, fertile land belongs. You know that many English persons have fair skins, blue eyes, and light hair; but perhaps you

HOUSES OF PARLIAMENT.

do not know that this sort of complexion comes from a brave seafaring people who conquered Britain some twelve or thirteen centuries ago. These were the *Saxons*, who came from a land on the other side of the North Sea, a spot near the river Elbe. They conquered the country from the Britons, a people who were not strong enough to keep it for themselves, and were therefore driven into out-of-the-way corners, among the hills of Cornwall and Wales, for instance, while the Saxons took the best of the land for themselves. It was named England after the *Angles*, a tribe allied to the Saxons, and who took part in the conquest. From these northern warriors we get some of our best national qualities; they were a brave, truth-telling people, who liked to work on steadily at whatever they took in hand until it was finished.

All English persons have not fair complexions, because we are a *mixed race*. Soon the Danes, another race of northern warriors, very like the Saxons, came for a share of the prize their neighbours had won. They also succeeded in conquering England, and settled along the eastern shores. Later still, William the Conqueror came with his Norman followers and won this country for himself in the battle of Hastings, 1066, after which many Normans came to live in England. Thus you see it is very difficult to tell whether an Englishman is descended from Normans, Saxons, Danes, or Britons, or even from Romans. The Saxons were never driven out by new invaders, and because they were the most numerous, and proved in the end the strongest people, we think of the English nation as descended chiefly from them.

Though each of the invading nations added new words to the stock, it is to the Saxons chiefly we owe the noble and beautiful English language. English is spoken all over the country, but several counties have curious dialects, which strangers find it difficult to understand. These differences of speech are, however, dying away, because people travel about a good deal from county to county now, and thus they forget the dialect of the district where they were born. People go about more now than formerly because it is easy to get from one end of England to the other; the whole country is covered with a network of railways, and but few English villages are more than five miles distant from a railway station. Nine main, or principal, lines reach out like long arms from London to the most distant parts of the country; and besides these there are endless branch lines, which connect scattered towns and villages with the main lines.

It is possible to reach the North of England, Newcastle, or Carlisle, by three of these main lines,—the *London and North-Western*, the *Great Northern*, and the *Midland*, each line taking, as its name shows, a somewhat different course.

To reach the towns of Devon and Cornwall, we journey by the *Great Western*; while the *Great Eastern* would take us to the towns of the eastern counties, Norwich, Yarmouth, Cambridge, &c. The destinations of the *London, Chatham, and Dover*, and the *London, Brighton and South Coast* lines are evident from their names; as are also the directions of the *South-Western* and the *South-Eastern* lines.

We are apt to think most of the convenience of railways for passengers, but perhaps their most important use is to bear goods to the ports from which they are shipped for foreign lands, or to the places at home where they may be wanted; and no doubt you have often noticed long "goods trains" laden with cattle or coal, iron, wool, or whatever the neighbourhood produces.

All goods do not, however, reach their destination by rail; it is cheaper to carry certain heavy articles by water, in barges drawn by horses, and for this purpose the numerous navigable rivers which England possesses are made use of. Rivers are navigable when their waters are deep and their beds are even, so that boats may glide smoothly along. Before railways were invented, it was found that such waterways were wanted in many places where there were no natural rivers deep enough to carry barges. Therefore many canals were made, that is, artificial channels connected with the rivers and filled with water from them; and by means of these, boats pass from one river to another, and thus carry goods from distant towns to ports at the mouths of the rivers.

Then, a good road leads to almost every spot in the country to which people are likely to journey for business or pleasure; so that the means of communication by road, railway, river, and canal, are excellent throughout England, no part of which is shut off from intercourse with the rest because there is no means of getting to it. More than half the people of England live in towns because in them great manufactures are carried on which afford work and wages to large numbers of people collected together in one spot. Thus, the clothing towns and the cotton and ironworking towns have a large population; so have the seaports, because in them also many persons can find employment; while London, which is both a great seaport and the seat of many manufactures, has a population of three and a half millions, as many inhabitants as are contained in the whole of Scotland! England and Wales together have a population of about 25 millions, and if these were evenly divided all over the country, there would be 340 persons to every square mile of land. But the farming districts do not contain nearly so many people in proportion to their size as do those parts of the country where there are many towns; while waste land and regions of moor and mountain have very few inhabitants indeed.

LESSON XIX.
IRELAND.

THE "Emerald Isle" is the most westerly of the British Isles. It owes this pretty and fanciful title to the fact that the grass is always green, or, at any rate, it has seldom the parched and brown look of English grass in a dry season. Ireland has always plenty of rain, because the west winds which blow off the Atlantic are full of watery vapour, which comes down in frequent showers; and these cause the verdant appearance for which the country is famous. For the same reason, more rain falls in the western counties of England than in the eastern; and because moist air never becomes quite so cold as dry air, Ireland, and the western counties of England, are, on the whole, warmer than the eastern counties. As a moist soil is good for grass, there are many pasture fields all over the country, and great numbers of cattle are fed; much of the butter made from their milk is exported to England. There is not much corn grown, partly because the soil is less suitable for corn than for grass; and partly because land must be carefully manured, and much labour and money must be spent upon it in various ways to make it produce good corn crops,—an outlay which the Irish peasant farmers are too poor to afford potatoes, however, are largely grown, and form the chief food of the people; failures in this crop have often been followed by frightful famines.

So much has Ireland suffered in this and other ways of late, that more than a third of her people have emigrated—dearly as they love their native land—to find work and wages in America or in Australia.

Oats are more largely grown than any other kind of corn, and, in the northern counties especially, oatmeal porridge is a good deal eaten.

You would think that because things often go badly with them, the Irish must be a sad and gloomy people; but, on the contrary, they are light-hearted and full of fun and jokes, excepting when trouble is pressing upon them. They are not a Saxon people like the English, but are *Celts*, allied to the ancient Britons and to the Welsh of the present day. Most of the people speak English, however, for Ireland has belonged to England for about seven centuries.

The people of Ulster, the northern province of Ireland, are partly of Saxon descent. King James I. of England settled a colony of Lowland Scots here, from whom many of the present inhabitants are descended; and they have made this north-eastern corner the richest and most prosperous part of the island. They brought with them, from their Scotch homes, the art of making linen, and this is still the most important manufacture of Ireland. There are large fields of the flax plant in these northern counties; it is grown for the fibres of the stalk, of which, after much steeping in water and various other processes, linen is made. The peasants may be seen at work in many of the cottages weaving linen in small hand-looms; they grow the flax themselves and prepare the fibres, and their wives and daughters spin the yarn. But most of the linen is made in the towns, from which rise tall mill-chimneys like those in the English cotton towns. Belfast and Drogheda are the most important linen-making places. Belfast is a large and busy seaport with a good harbour, where cotton as well as linen is manufactured.

LESSON XX.
IRELAND.
PART II.

THE cliffs on the coast of Antrim—the county in which Belfast is situated—are very remarkable, They are made of a rock called basalt, which is dark and hard, and heavy as iron; and these hard rocks have been worn by the waves into columns that look as if they had been carved by human hands. The cliffs of Fair Head are 600 feet high; but the great wonder of this coast is the Giant's Causeway. This curious pier stretches for a thousand feet into the sea, and is made of many five-or-six-sided columns, packed close together, fitting in with one another perfectly, and more even and regular than man could make them. Lough Neagh, in Antrim, is the largest lake in Ireland, and, indeed, in the British Isles; it has the curious property of *petrifying*, or gradually coating over with stony substance, whatever is thrown into it. Ireland has a good many lakes, which are called *loughs* here, while in Scotland they are termed *lochs*. There are three large loughs, Allen, Ree, and Dearg, in the course of the Shannon, which is the largest of the Irish rivers. The seaport town of Limerick stands at its mouth.

The beautiful lake country of Ireland, which is a little like our English lake district in Cumberland and Westmorland, is in county Kerry, at the south west corner of the island. Here are the three famous lakes of Killarney, on whose wooded banks the arbutus grows freely; the lakes are studded with fairy isles, and are hemmed in by mountains, in some places rugged and awful, in others clothed with trees and grass. The other two counties of Ireland which are remarkable for their scenery are Galway, in the west, which is wild and much broken into by the sea; and Wicklow on the east, which has hills and lovely river valleys. The Vale of Avoca is famous in song. You will notice that these three picturesque counties—that is, counties where hill, valley, and water make pictures pleasant to the eye—are all upon the sea-coast.

Carry your eye round the map of Ireland, and you will see there are various other mountain ranges near the coast; you can count six or more distinct chains, while, running inland, there are only the Slieve Bloom Mountains, which reach as far as King's County. None of these mountain ranges are high, and they are usually covered to the top with grass, upon which sheep and cattle feed. There are a great many goats also in the hilly districts, which are much valued for their milk.

The middle of Ireland is a wide plain; it is rather high and in some places hilly, and yet it consists for the most part of soaking *bogs* which cover more than a third part of the country. They form a dreary waste which, in many places, it is not safe to cross, because the ground is filled with stagnant water. After much rain the bogs sometimes burst and flood the surrounding land. The largest of these wastes is the Bog of Allen.

Although men cannot build upon the bogs, or till them, they have a certain use. There is not much coal in Ireland, and what there is, is not of a good kind; and there are very few trees indeed, so the people cannot use wood for fuel. They cut sods from the bogs and pile them in stacks to dry; and these peat sods, which burn with a peculiar smell, are what the peasants make their fires of. The bogs seems to consist a good deal of decayed forests, which once covered a great part of the country.

As most of the inhabitants are engaged in tilling the ground, Ireland has but few large towns. Dublin, the capital, is a handsome city which stands on the east coast where the Liffey falls into Dublin Bay. It has a beautiful park. Poplin—a stuff made of a mixture of silk and wool—is manufactured here.

Cork, which has a very fine harbour, is the next town of importance; it is a busy seaport, and exports pigs and bullocks, pork and butter, besides a great deal of tinned meat, which is prepared in the town.

QUESTIONS ON THE MAP OF THE BRITISH ISLES.

1. What waters divide the island of Great Britain from the Continent?
2. What countries have coasts on the further side of the North Sea?
3. The island of Great Britain contains three countries; name them. Which is the most northerly? The most westerly? The most important?
4. A range of hills partly divides England from Scotland; name it.
5. What large island lies to the west of Great Britain? What waters separate these two islands?
6. How is England separated from France? Name an island, two or three headlands, and two or three bays on the English shore of this channel.
7. What strait connects the English Channel with the North Sea? Sailing northward from this strait, what is the first headland we pass?
8. What is the first large opening on the eastern coast? Name the great town upon this river.
9. Name any seaboard towns on the coast of the round eastern shoulder.
10. What rivers flow into the Wash?
11. What name is given to the country round the Wash?
12. What is the next large opening to the north? What rivers form the Humber? What point is at its mouth?
13. Name another bold headland further north.
14. Name any English rivers which flow into the North Sea, north of the Humber.
15. What town stands where England and Scotland meet?
16. Sailing north, what large eastuary do we shortly pass? What town stands on the Forth?
17. Name two other rivers with seaport towns at their mouths on the east coast of Scotland.
18. Rounding the shoulder and sailing westward, what firth do we enter?
19. Rounding the north-eastern point of Scotland and sailing through the Pentland Firth, what islands have we on our right?
20. What other group lies further to the north-east?
21. What waters are we in as we coast the north of Scotland? As we sail down the west?
22. Bailing down the channel called the "Minch," what islands have we on our right?
23. How would you describe the western coast of Scotland?
24. Name the five largest islands which lie close to the coast. Name the largest openings.
25. Between what two openings might we pass through Scotland in a boat, by means of lakes and a canal?
26. What large city stands upon the Clyde?
27. Name half-a-dozen Scotch headlands, stating which coast they are upon.

28. What firth penetrates some way between England and Scotland on the west?

29. What English headland stretches furthest into the Irish Sea?

30. What island in the Irish Sea is almost equally distant from England, Scotland, and Ireland?

31. Name any English rivers which flow into the Irish Sea. A large seaport on the Mersey.

32. Having passed the Dee, what country do we coast as we sail southward?

33. Through what strait may we pass so as to have a large island on our right? Name the island.

34. What name is given to the waters between Wales and Ireland?

35. Name the two Welsh headlands which stretch furthest into the sea. What bay is between these?

36. What channel enters the land between South Wales and a part of England? What river is this channel the estuary of? Name a seaport at its mouth.

37. Sailing out of the Bristol Channel and southward, what is the last point of English ground we come to?

38. Name any mountains in Scotland north of the Caledonian Canal. What would you say of the whole country?

39. What range of mountains crosses the country south of this canal?

40. What other pan of the country ia mountainous? Name any of the hill ranges.

41. Name half-a-dozen towns in the interior of Scotland. Say where they are.

42. What parts of England are mountainous? What parts are flat?

43. Name the mountain-chain which runs from the borders of Scotland nearly to the middle of England.

44. What rivers rise in these mountains and flow east or west?

45. Name any towns in this northern part of the country, and say on which side of the mountains they lie.

46. What name is given to the mountain-chains of Wales.

47. Name any towns in the flat middle part of England. In the flat eastern counties.

48. Name any hill ranges in the south.

49. Name half-a-dozen towns in the southern counties.

50. Name five or six capes round the coast of Ireland, and three or four bays.

51. Where are the mountains of Ireland, near the coast, or in the interior? Name any mountain-chains.

52. Name the six largest rivers of Ireland. Which of these form lakes in-their courses? Name any of these lakes.

53. What Bog occupies much of the centre of Ireland?

54. Name half-a-dozen seaport towns on the coast.

LESSON XXL
FRANCE.

IN "the pleasant land of France" do most English people enjoy, for the first time, the wonder and delight of being in a foreign country. A sail of an hour or so brings you to Calais, where you find your English tongue of little service. Or you may take the boat for Boulogne, pleasantest of watering-places, where the ladies and gentlemen bathe together in gay costumes, and where the charming Frenchwomen go about in their neat dresses and becoming white caps, which are much prettier than hats or bonnets.

Or, arriving at the quaint seaport town of Dieppe, you may watch the old women in their high Normandy caps as they stroll, knitting in hand, along the quay. You are inclined to think the solemn-looking caps they wear must have something to do with the cleverness of the children; how else should they speak French so well, when we find it so troublesome to learn?

Did you ever see such piles of cherries as are for sale along the quay?—to be bought at the rate of a penny a pound. It is plain that Normandy is, like the county of Kent, a cherry-growing district.

The name "Normandy" makes us feel at home in this strange land. We remember that our Norman kings came from here, and that, for nearly four centuries, Normandy and the whole western half of France belonged, more or less, to the English kings, who called themselves kings of France also. This was an unhappy state of things, which led to constant wars between the two countries. Indeed, the last century of English possession was one long "Hundred Years' War", in which two of the English kings, Edward III. and Henry V., gained some famous victories. We are still proud to remember the battles of Cressy, Poictiers, and Agincourt.

Let us go on to the ancient city of Rouen, where a thing was done which English people are ashamed and sad to remember. In the market-place of Rouen Joan of Arc, the brave and gentle peasant girl whose courage and faith in God had saved her country, was burnt as a witch by the English. "Jesus!" she cried, when the cruel flames reached her tender flesh; and an English soldier who heard her said "We are lost—we have burned a saint! "

The English cause was lost. The war went on a few years longer, and everywhere the English were defeated, until nothing was left of their vast possessions but the town of Calais.

Rouen, which has a cathedral and a very beautiful church of St. Ouen, is sometimes called "the Manchester of France," because cotton goods are made here. But a single look at the quiet, bright old city—many of whose shops and warehouses can hardly be distinguished from dwelling-houses—would show that cotton-spinning in France is by no means the great industry it is with ourselves. France is not so great a manufacturing country as England: half the people in England live in towns, where they work in mills or foundries in some manufacturing *centre*, where many people are gathered together. In France, only a third of the inhabitants live in towns; the greater number are employed in tilling the land. The north of France, north of a line drawn across the country from the mouth of the Loire; is the busiest part, and here are many towns where iron goods, linen, cotton, and woollen stuffs are made. Lille is a busy manufacturing town. *Cambric* is made at Cambrai, and Valenciennes is famous for its beautiful lace.

This northern part of France is like the south of England, only it is a, little warmer in the summer and colder in the winter. Corn and apples, pears, and cherries, grow here as in the southern counties of England; the people drink cider, they keep cows and make butter, and they rear an immense quantity of poultry. The French do not eat nearly so much meat as we eat; they live a good deal on wheaten bread, made into curiously shaped loaves, which are sometimes round like a hoop, and sometimes are more than a yard long. They also use many chickens, and a great quantity of eggs. Not that Madame would serve a simple boiled egg as we do in England; in a few minutes she tosses up a delicious *omelette*, such as only a Frenchwoman can make—that is, a sort of pancake turnover, with sweets or savoury herbs inside. But the *potage*, or soup, is the everyday food of the people, of which they never seem to tire; a little pan of it is always simmering on the little charcoal stove, ready for breakfast, dinner, or supper. These soups cost little, as they are made for the most part of vegetables, and the French are very clever in contriving many varieties.

It is well Madame should know bow to cook en excellent dinner out of little, for the French peasants are poor. The land is cut up into many small farms, for the father's property is divided at his death equally among his children; and this is why we constantly see, in France, patches of wheat no bigger than an English cabbage garden. Very hard work it is to gain a living out of these small farms; father, mother, and children all have to do field work, and it tells upon the women, who grow brown and wizened and old before their time.

But we must quit the country folk, and hasten to Paris, *the* city of France, and the brightest and gayest of towns, where the people seem to live out of doors, sipping coffee or wine at little round tables on the broad side-walks of the *boulevards*, as many of the wide streets are called. Lively and pleasure-loving as the people are, Paris is not an idle town. Jewelry and watches, delicious sweetmeats and perfumes, furniture, gloves, elegant robes and bonnets, which go all over the world to set the fashions—these, and a hundred other costly and beautiful things, are made by the deft fingers of the Parisians. We have no room to describe the palaces, parks, and picture galleries of the splendid city; nor the glorious cathedral and other ancient buildings, which stand upon an island in the Seine; nor the bridges which span the beautiful river. We must leave Paris, and journey further south. A second line, drawn from the mouth of the Garonne right across the country, encloses Middle France. This is a pleasant, sunshiny land, where the vine is grown everywhere, either trained along the ground or upon poles, as hops are in England. The grape-gathering is a pretty sight, and the season is one of much mirth and festivity. Wine is made from the grapes, much of which is exported, but a good deal is drunk by the people, who use wine as commonly as the English use beer. French people, however, seldom drink too much.

Delightful as the climate is here, the people have occasion to

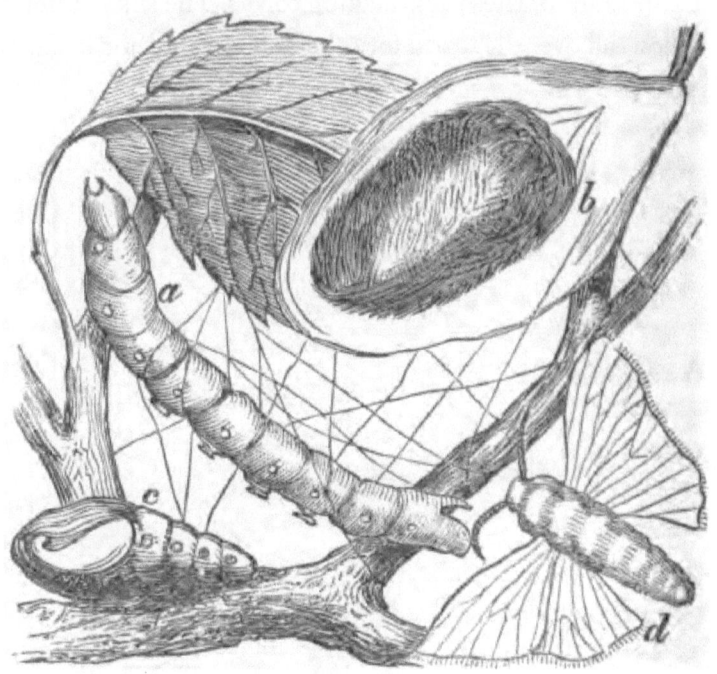

SILKWORM.

dread the tremendous hail-storms, which every year destroy many of the tender grapes. These storms, and the floods which overflow the valley of the Loire when the snows of the Cevennes melt, often cause much distress among the inhabitants.

Southern France is a still warmer, sunnier region. Here the people make little butter, and do all their cooking with oil; the oil they use is pressed out of the fruit of the olive-tree, which grows only in warm, sunny lands. The mulberry-tree, too, is largely grown in this part of France for its leaves which are the favourite food of the dainty silkworm. To take care of these worms, and reel the silk off their cocoons, is the principal work of the people in this part of France. In the towns of the beautiful warm Rhone valley the people are employed in manufacturing the silk; Lyons is the most important of these silk-making towns. The silks of France are famous all over the world for their good quality and beautiful colours.

LESSON XXLI.
SPAIN AND PORTUGAL.

IF the south of France is warm and sunny, how delightful must these two lands of Southern Europe be! Two countries they are, but the map shows that the same rivers flow, and the same mountain chains run, through them both; we see, too, that together they form a great peninsula, separated from Africa only by narrow straits which open into the Mediterranean.

Just within the Straits is a tongue of land, upon which is a great rock mountain with so steep a fall to the sea that it cannot be climbed. This rock is made into a fortress, bristling all over with guns, to hold which, holes and passages have been cut in the solid stone; and this great fortress is the key to the Mediterranean.

British ships, however, may enter the Straits freely, because the fortress of GIBRALTAR, with its thousand huge guns, does not belong to Spain at all, but to England; and many English soldiers man the guns and keep the forts. In times of peace, the soldiers are glad to amuse themselves sometimes by going after the little monkeys which dwell in the high cliffs; this is the only part of Europe where these amusing creatures are to be found in a wild state.

As we may venture through the Straits, let us take ship, and collect a cargo of the good things of Spain. We must stop on our way at Oporto, and take in a stock of port wine; for the Douro, upon which this large town stands, flows through a famous wine-growing district. The vineyards stretch upon either side of the river for many miles; and thousands of women and children flock thither for the vintage, to gather the ripe grapes; and thousands of men are employed to tread them, in order to press out the juice.

We cannot pass by Lisbon either without stopping to see the capital of Portugal; and, as we enter the wide mouth of the Tagus,

GIBRALTAR.

a swarm of little boats gathers round our vessel, laden high with oranges, figs, grapes, pomegranates, and other delicious and beautiful fruits, which they are eager to sell. The bright buildings of the town, high above upon bills, look very pretty from the harbour; but when we enter, the narrow and dirty streets are disappointing. Lisbon was nearly destroyed by a terrible earthquake which took place more than a century ago: public buildings and many streets of houses were thrown down, and nearly sixty thousand persons perished.

Round by Spain now; we sail some way up the Guadalquivir to the town of Seville, where we lay in great Seville oranges for marmalade. Through the Straits we go, and, ho! for "Malaga raisins, best of raisins under the sun."

We have forgotten, however, to take in our stock of *sherry* wine at Cadiz, whither it is sent from Xeres, where an immense quantity is made.

We cannot stop everywhere; we must pass by large seaports, and towns famous in story, in which there are strange and beautiful buildings. But we keep as near shore as we can, and are delighted to see banks of brilliant flowers, and groves of glowing fruits; and say! surely those are palm-trees, the real palms of the East, which we have long known in pictures. The bright-gleaming oranges and lemons are varied by darker groves of mulberry-trees: for the useful little silkworm seems to enjoy the pleasant air of these sea-side plains, and more silk is produced here than in any other country of Europe excepting Italy. Most of it, however, is sent to France to be manufactured.

How pretty the villages look—the houses nestling among fruit-trees and flowers, and coloured, sometimes pink, sometimes blue, for bright colours look well here, the more so as many of the trees bear dull, dark-green leaves. The peasants like bright clothes also, and the crimson sashes or waistbands of the men and the bright petticoats of the women flash gaily in the open-air dance with which they love to end the day.

But we must get on to the busy seaport town of Barcelona, and complete our cargo with nuts, "Barcelona nuts," which have been gathered in the great forests that cover so large a part of Northern Spain. Sweet chestnuts, too, abound in these forests, and the people cook and eat them as freely as we do potatoes.

We have finished our voyage now, and say to ourselves, What a delightful land is Spain! How full of delicious things and pleasant pots and happy people! But Spain is rather like a house which hangs up handsome blinds and curtains, and has dreary and empty rooms within. All the middle of the country, away from the pleasant plains of the coast, is a high dreary tableland, with hardly a tree to afford shelter from the bitter cold of winter, or the burning heat of the summer sun. It is crossed, as the map shows, from east to west, by ranges of mountains, which are dreary as itself; rivers flow between the mountain ranges, but they dry up or get very shallow in the summer when they are most wanted. Madrid, the capital of

Spain, stands upon this plain, and is the highest city in Europe: it is a dull enough town, except when the Spanish women take their evening walks: no other ladies know how to move with such stately grace, and very pretty they look in the black lace mantillas they commonly wear instead of bonnets.

LESSON XXIII.
ITALY.

LIKE a picture, like a poem, like a dream of pleasant things, is the very name of sunny, beautiful *Italy*; rather, this name, as with magical power, calls up a succession of shifting pictures, pleasing visions.

We close our eyes, and, behold,—

> "A glorious city in the sea;
> The sea is in the broad, the narrow streets,
> Ebbing and flowing; and the salt sea-weed
> Clings to the marble of her palaces!
> No tread of men, no footsteps to and fro,
> Tread to her gates: the path lies o'er the sea."

Here is, indeed, a strange silent city, where the sound of wheels is never heard, for the streets are water, and the carriages are long black boats with a rower at either end, and what looks like the body of a carriage in the middle. These are *gondolas*; and are to be seen perpetually skimming the broad, the narrow way, bearing passengers or goods from street to street. The "Lady of Lombardy," the "City of the Sea," owes her beauty to the misfortunes of her founders. Many centuries ago, the clever and industrious citizens of Padua, and other towns on the Adriatic, were driven from their homes by At'tila, king of the Huns. There are at the head of the Adriatic about a hundred little islands, formed of mud and sand swept down by the rivers which flow through Northern Italy. These islands are Surrounded by shallow water, and between them are many narrow channels. The Vene'ti, driven from the mainland, settled themselves upon these islands, and there founded a city in the midst of the waters. It was slow work. For years, the settlers could barely keep the wolf from the door. But they built ships and traded; by-and-by, they gathered riches, raised splendid palaces of marble on one little island after another, and built the grand square of St. Mark with the remarkable bell-tower. Of these poor little isles, the refuge of outcasts, they made a great merchant city—beautiful Venice!

Look again; there is a yellow rapid river, and, beyond, a cluster of seven hills; upon the bills rise the buildings of a great city, and among these are gardens and vineyards and olive-yards. How many of the buildings seem to be churches! Churches they are; for the city is *Rome*, which has as many churches, all but one, as there are days in the year; and, amongst them, St. Peter's, the largest church in the world. The streets swarm with priests who serve these churches; and there are, at certain seasons, a great many visitors in the city, who go to Rome, partly to see the grand shows of the Romish Church and the Pope who is the head of it. But still more do educated people care to see the remains of ancient Rome—the ruins of buildings larger and grander than any the world has since produced.

How the beggars swarm and torment the visitors, and what crowds of pretty boys and girls lie about the steps of the buildings, nibbling long sticks of maccaroni! How dirty and narrow many of the streets are! It is pleasant to think that, now, all Italy has a king of its own, who will try to help the people into better ways. The children will, we hope, be gathered into schools; and the streets will be made clean. Rome, which has for centuries belonged to the Pope, is now the capital of the new kingdom of Italy.

We avoid the *Campagna*, a deserted plain to the north of Rome, where there is hardly a hut, or even a tree to be seen. The grass looks green and rich, and there are many cattle and sheep feeding upon it; the sickly-looking shepherds, wrapped in blankets, walk about upon high stilts. A way of amusing themselves? Not at all; a foul air, *malaria*, rises from the swampy flats, and those who breathe this air fall ill of fever or ague. The shepherds use stilts to raise them, as the air is worst near the ground. This low unhealthy plain stretches, under different names, nearly all along the western coast. We keep inland, within sight of the mountains, the long chain of the Apennines, which goes all through Italy, and is covered in many parts with forests of chestnuts. On the lower slopes, there are mulberry groves for the silkworms, for more silk is produced in Italy than in any other country of Europe; there are endless vineyards; and there are whole groves of oranges!

"See Naples and then die," says the Neapolitan proverb, as if nothing were left worth seeing after this fair city. And what can be lovelier to look upon than the white buildings of the city rising on a hill-side among orchards, vineyards, and groves of oranges, between the blue sky of Italy and the blue Sea by which Naples stands! Within, there is a wonderful hubbub; the streets are crowded, for workers in every trade, shoemakers, carpenters, smiths, weavers, do their work out of doors. That is, if any work can go on while everybody is talking at the top of his voice, and gesticulating with hands and arms to make his meaning the plainer; the wonder is, who listens? The streets of Naples are paved with blocks of a curious substance, namely, *lava*. Lava is the melted matter—which becomes hard as it cools—that is thrown out of the hole or *crater* of a volcano. Only a few miles from Naples is Vesuvius, a famous volcano whose fires are often burning; then, streams of lava flow down its sides, and clouds of thick vapour rise from its monster chimney. Sometimes lava and fiery cinders come in such quantities as to spread over the plain at the foot of the mountain; in the old Roman days, the two cities of Herculaneum and Pompeii, which stood at the base of Vesuvius, were buried, the one under ashes, the other under lava, before the people had time to escape. Italy has another volcano, Mount Etna, which is in the island of Sicily.

We must leave Italy without seeing the beautiful and fertile wheat-growing plain in the north, the Plain of Lombardy, which is watered by the rapid river Po.

LESSON XXIV.
SWITZERLAND.

Is there any treat to equal a first visit to Switzerland? The very name calls up, not a country where people live in towns and work at trades for their living, but green, sunny valleys, blue lakes, snow-capped mountains, fields of ice, and pleasant, merry travelling over difficult ways.

The "playground of Europe" the little country is called; and no people swarm there to play through a happy holiday more than the English.

Let us enter where the Rhine leaves Switzerland, at the pleasant town of Basle. We may chance to see a stork's nest or two on the roofs of the houses on our way to the *Three Kings*, which hotel we choose because its windows overhang the Rhine. How the river rushes along!—if such a stately, rapid sweep may be called "rushing." On, on, it goes, with a continual strong flow, while we gaze with awe and delight; and in thought we follow it back to the high Alps, where it gathers, not its waters only, but its force. We all know how fast and how easily we run downhill.

We must not linger at Basle; let us go on to Geneva, the bright capital of Switzerland, where "Geneva's blue waters" spread before us, and the mighty Blanc, the highest of the Alps, nearly five times as high as any mountain in England, towers in the distance. It is partly a French mountain now, though we always think of it as part of Switzerland.

Or, better still, let us away to the heart of the Alps to Lucerne, resting on the margin of its beautiful lake, and girdled by chains of snowy Alps. Upon one of the shadowy bays of the lake stands the chapel of William Tell, the hero of Switzerland, who is said to have made the Swiss a free nation.

SWISS LAKE.

From the shore of Lucerne rises the big, swelling Rigi. If we are not good mountain climbers, we may ascend by the marvellous railway which goes to the very summit of the mountain. Of course, we must see the sun rise. At three o'clock in the morning, perhaps, when we are comfortably asleep—for there is an hotel at the top of the mountain—we are startled by a ringing blast from the long Alpine horn with which the mountaineers call their cattle home. Sleepy as we are, we tumble out of bed; we must see the sun rise, and he waits for nobody. A motley crowd we are, wrapped in whatever came uppermost, and we have time to look at one another, for the sun has not yet bestirred himself; the world is waiting for him in a clear, still light. At last the eastern sky grows rosy; the white maiden-mountains flush all over at the coming of their lord with a pink blush like nothing so much as that which pleasure kindles in the face of a child. More glorious, more golden grows the sky; the rim rises slowly from behind the mountains; by-and-by the great round orb has fully risen, and is mounting high in the heavens.

We are in no hurry to go in; the Alps lie before us, the snowy Alps of the Bernese Oberland, chain behind chain, peak beyond peak, white and gleaming in the early light. These are the real mountains we have imagined all our lives, whose heads reach so high that they get into cold, strange air, where water becomes ice and mist is converted into snow, and the snow never wholly melts away.

We can pick out one and another shape we know. There is the Jungfrau (the maiden), and there is the great St. Gothard, which has just been pierced in a wonderful way for a railway into Italy. How lovely the valleys are, with villages nestling in them, which might be play-things, so tiny they look—toy-houses which you might carry in your pinafore. And the lakes!—fully a dozen of them you may count, lying like shining mirrors in the valleys. The Rigi itself is full of delight. There are the handsome, friendly cows, each with its great bell about its neck, and the goats, and the strange Alpine flowers. The most beautiful of these is the lovely little gentian, each flower growing by itself, set on the green earth as stars are set in the sky, and so blue, so very blue; bluer than the sky, or the eyes of a child, or than any blue thing you have seen.

But if we can climb well, we shall not be content with the Rigi. We get a guide and an alpenstock, that is, a long stick to steady our steps, and away for the high Alps; we must see the *glaciers*. What are glaciers? They are great fields of ice, or rather, of frozen snow, sometimes fifteen or sixteen miles long and a mile or two across, of which there are hundreds in the high valleys of the Alps. The high valleys being filled, the great mass of ice slides very slowly down towards the low valley at the foot of the mountain. The glacier is, in fact, a slow-moving river of ice, by which the snow, for which there is no longer room on the mountain peaks or in the high valleys, reaches the low plains, where it will be converted into water. Very curious these glaciers look; sometimes they are like a smooth summer sea, and sometimes the ice rises in great jagged heaps, and looks like the ocean suddenly frozen in the midst of a storm. Here and there are frightful cracks in these ice-rivers, chasms which reach down hundreds of feet, so thick is the ice, and many an unwary traveller has slipped into these dread ravines and been heard of no more.

The partial thaw of the snow in the spring causes another fearful danger. The snow on the mountaintops is loosened, and rolls down the sides of the mountains in immense quantities and with

A GLACIER.

great force; and these fearful *avalanches* sometimes bury whole villages in the valleys below deep beneath a snowy covering. We must not linger among the Alps, nor must we stop to say much about the brave and hardy Swiss. Dearly they love their beautiful native land, but the mountains and the lakes take up a great deal of room, and leave them but little land to till; therefore, though they are very industrious people, many Swiss have to leave their homes and seek work in foreign countries, but always with the hope of returning when they have earned enough to keep them in Switzerland. The watches made in Switzerland, Geneva watches, are well known everywhere.

LESSON XXV.
GERMANY.

GERMANY ie a very large country, and, in many ways, is one of the most important in Europe. It is a country made up of many countries, or states, which speak the same language and care about the same things, and have lately agreed to place themselves under the King of Prussia, who is therefore the Emperor of Germany. His eldest son, Prince Frederick William, has married our Princess Royal, the eldest daughter of our Queen. This is not the only tie which binds us to the Germans. Strange as their language sounds to us, many of their words are just like our own; they love their homes as English people do, care for books and study, perhaps, more than we do, are truthful and industrious, and are fair and ruddy, and not very unlike English people in appearance. Is there any reason why the English and the Germans should be alike in so many ways? There is a sort of cousinship between the nations, for they belong to the same *race*; that is to say, both the Germans and the English are descended from the same brave people. The Saxons who conquered Britain many centuries ago, came, in the first place, in their war-ships from what is now a part of Germany—the part lying near the river Elbe, upon the North Sea.

But when you are in Germany, you say to yourself, not, How like England it is! but, How different! It is hard, at first, to say wherein the difference lies. Very much the same sort of things grow in the two countries; apples and pears, cherries and plums, corn, potatoes, and cabbage. The Germans eat a great deal of cabbage, made into a salt, sour pickle called sauerkraut, which foreigners think very nasty. Cotton, linen, and woollen stuffs, and iron goods, are made as with us: but here we come to one difference. Cotton is manufactured in one part of England, iron in another, wool in a third. In Germany it is not so; each of the large towns has all these and other manufactures carried on in it. We see much that strikes us as new in the towns; they are seldom so large and crowded as our busy English towns. The best streets are often very wide, and in the middle are walks delightfully shaded by fine trees with seats under them where the women sit and knit: German women knit a great deal.

In the evening, it is pleasant to see the man and his wife with their heads well out of an open window. Do not imagine they have come to look at something, and will pop in again in a minute; on the contrary, they may stay there for an hour. Notice the red cushions for their elbows, made to fit the window-seat, and you will see they mean to be comfortable. The houses are usually very high, and each family has, not a nice little house for a home, as in England, but a single floor in one of these high houses.

Another thing that strikes us is, how much the German people think of the education of their children. They seem to think it just as important that the children should go to school as that the fathers should go to work; and you see scores of little lads and maidens, satchel on back, trotting off in the morning to be in good time for eight o'clock school.

Berlin is the capital of Prussia. Its principal street, *Unter den Linden* (under the lime-trees), is divided into five pleasant, shady avenues by chestnut, lime, and other trees. You are struck by the number of soldiers here, on parade or walking about. Prussia is what is called a great military power; that is, a country which has many soldiers. Indeed, every man has to spend three years of his life as a soldier, that he may be able to fight for his country should he be wanted.

Beautiful china is made in Berlin, as in some other towns of the Empire; the most beautiful and costly is the kind called Dresden china.

A sail up the Rhine takes us through the prettiest part of Germany. What a delightful sail it is!

Let us take the Rhine steamer at Cologne: this is a rather large town where Eau de Cologne is made, and where there is one of the most beautiful cathedrals in the world; it has been six hundred years in building, and is only now finished. Having seen this famous church we hasten on board, and up the beautiful river. How broad and stately it is! though much less rapid here than when we last met it at Basle. What strange-looking craft is this, laden with felled trees, and with rough little houses as well as women and children upon it? It is a raft; the trees of the forest are roughly fastened together thus, and set to float down stream in charge of men who often take their families with them. The raft will at last reach a port where it will be taken to pieces, that the timber may be sold. But we must use our eyes; we are nearing Bonn and getting into the most beautiful part of the river. Here and there either bank rises into a high cliff, crowned with the ruins of an ancient castle; for many castles stand on each side of the Rhine, and stories belong to them all. Almost every bend of the river, every rock, every island, has its story, so that a sail down the Rhine is like a delightful book of fairy tales. Up the banks, even to the tops of the high hills, the vine is grown carefully; not an inch of ground is wasted; and where the hill-side is too steep to support the plants, a sort of shelf or terrace is made for them. Words will not help us to imagine half the beauty and delight of this Rhine river, the vine-clad banks, the craggy heights, the mountains, drawing close up to the river, the cosy comers where the pretty towns nestle, the dark steep cliffs, the jagged ruins of the old keeps, which look down on us as if they would say that they and the Rhine were there centuries before we came into the world! No wonder the Germans think much of their beautiful river, and delight to sing its praises.

LESSON XXVI.
HOLLAND.

HOLLAND is an extraordinary little country. It is crowded with busy people, and has large seaports, and ships which trade with many lands. Much of the country consists of meadow-land, and many cows are kept, from whose milk butter and cheese are made. The Dutch have some manufactures; they make the kind of linen we call "holland", manufacture a certain kind of spirit, and build ships, both for their own use and to sell to other countries. They grow flowers largely, especially tulips and hyacinths, the bulbs of which they export. All these things, and many more, they do; but none of these is the principal business of the Dutch people. What that is, you would never guess. "I strive, and keep my head above water," is the motto of one division of the country, and this is exactly the principal business of the Dutch—to keep their heads above water; above real water that would drown them and their cities and all belonging to them, and make of Holland a South Sea; to match the North Sea which washes it.

They have not always been successful; look on the map, and you will see a great opening called the Zuyder Zee, which means south sea. There, and in other parts of Holland, the sea has had the best of the fight; it poured in over towns and villages, and destroyed many thousands of people, who were going about their work without fear, forgetful of the terrible foe upon their borders. But what can these Dutch people do? What is the use of fighting with such a foe as the sea? If they were to withdraw from the conflict for a day, all might be over with them; so sentinels keep watch day and night, as when armies are fighting; and if they see the foe advance, an alarm is sounded, upon which every man must rush from his business or his bed to join in the battle.

This is how it is: Holland is the lowest part of the great plain of Middle Europe. So low is it, that the very rivers flow far above the level of the land, and have to be kept in their beds by huge banks of earth called dykes. If a dyke give way, the river must rush out and flood the land. Nor is this the only source of peril; being so low, much of Holland was at one time under water; the people had not room to live; so they determined to get rid of the water. They built channels, or canals, to hold it, and they made pumps worked by windmills to pump the low-lying water up into these canals. So successful were these efforts that, where wide lakes once lay, there are now fields of very green grass, with dykes and windmills all round them, bordering the canals which carry the water to the sea. But if *these* dykes were to burst, the water would rush out, and the green fields be once more flooded.

Worse danger than all the rest, Holland lies lower than the *sea*. Along part of the coast, there are sandhills which help to keep it out, but in other parts the people have raised tremendous granite walls and dykes, huge and strong. For the west wind drives the sea in upon Holland, and it is hard for any works of men to stand against it. Think of it; think of standing inside such a sea-wall and hearing the sea roar without, high above your head, with nothing but the wall between you and death. No wonder that looking after their dykes is the principal business of the Dutch.

Have you heard of the little boy who lived in Haarlem—a boy of eight—who saved his town by a "golden deed"?

Grass and wild flowers grow upon the dykes, trees are planted upon the tops of them, and they are broad enough at the top to form pleasant roads.

This little boy was hastening home one evening, just as the sun was setting. "Just as he was bracing himself for a run, he was startled by the sound of trickling water. Whence did it come? He looked up and saw a small hole in the dyke through which a tiny stream was flowing. Any child in Holland will shudder at the thought of a leak in the dyke; the boy understood the danger at a glance. That little hole, if the water were allowed to trickle through, would soon be a large one, and a terrible flood would be the result.

"Quick as a flash he saw his duty. Throwing away his flowers, the boy clambered up the height, until he reached the hole. His chubby little finger was thrust in almost before he knew it. The flowing was stopped! 'Ah!' he thought, with a chuckle of boyish delight, 'the waters must stay back now! Haarlem shall not be drowned while I am here.'

"This was all very well at first, but the night was falling fast, chill vapours filled the air. Our little hero began to tremble with cold and fear. He shouted loudly; he screamed 'Come here! come here!' but no one came. The cold grew more intense, a numbness, beginning in the tired little finger, crept over his hand and arm, and soon his whole body was filled with pain. He shouted again, 'Will no one come? mother! mother!' Alas! his mother had already locked the doors, and had quite resolved to scold him in the morning, for spending the night with his blind old friend without her permission. He tried to whistle, perhaps some straggling boy might hear the signal; but his teeth chattered so, it was impossible.

"The moon looked down upon that small lonely form, sitting upon a stone half-way up the dyke. His head was bent, but he was not asleep, for every now and then one restless hand rubbed freely the outstretched arm that seemed fastened to the dyke, and often the pale, tearful face turned quickly at some real or fancied sound.

"If he drew away that tiny finger, the waters would rush forth, and never stop until they bad swept over the town. No, he would hold it there till daylight—if he lived! He was not very sure of living. What did this strange buzzing mean? and then the knives that seemed pricking and piercing him from head to foot? He was not certain now that he could draw his finger away, even if he wished to.

"At daybreak, a clergyman, returning from the bedside of a sick man, thought he heard groans as he walked along on the top of the dyke. Bending, he saw, far down the side, a child who seemed to be writhing with pain.

"'Hi!' cried he in astonishment; 'What are you doing there, boy?'

"'I am keeping the water from running out,' was the simple answer of the little hero. 'Tell them to come quickly.'

"It is needless to add that they did come quickly, and that the little hero was relieved of his hard post. But the town was safe: and the safety of it and of all its inhabitants was due to his brave endurance."

Did you ever hear so grand a story? Does it nearly make you wish there were such dykes in England, so that some little English child, perhaps yourself, might save his country thus?

LESSON XXVII
SWEDEN AND NORWAY.

THE Scandinavian peninsula includes the two countries of Norway and Sweden. A range of rugged mountains runs from end to end of the peninsula, filling up nearly the whole of Norway. On the eastern side, this mountain chain has a rather long and gradual slope, so that Sweden is a comparatively flat country. In Norway, the mountains approach so close to the coast that the sea makes its way into the curious narrow valleys with steep walls of rock thousands of feet high; and where there might be fields with grazing cattle, there is *sea* between the mountains.

"Every one who has looked at the map of Norway must have been struck with the singular character of its coast. On the map it looks so jagged, such a strange mixture of land and sea, that it appears as if there must be a perpetual struggle between the two—the sea striving to inundate the land, and the land pushing itself out into the sea, till it ends in their dividing the region between them. On the spot, however, this coast is very sublime.

"The long straggling promontories are mountainous towering ridges of rock, springing up in precipices from the water; while the bays between them, instead of being rounded with shelving sandy shores, on which the sea tumbles its waves, as in bays of our coast, are, in fact, long, narrow valleys, filled with sea, instead of being laid out in fields and meadows.

"The high rocky banks shelter these deep bays (called fiords) from almost every wind; so that their waters are usually as still as those of a lake. For days and weeks together, they reflect each separate tree-top of the pine forests which clothe the mountain sides, the mirror only being broken by the leap of some sportive fish, or the oars of the boatman as he goes to inspect the sea-fowl from islet to islet of the fiord, or carries out his nets or his rod to catch the sea-trout, or char, or cod, or herrings, which abound in their seasons on the coast of Norway.

"It is difficult to say whether these fiords are the most beautiful in summer or in winter. In summer, they glitter with golden sunshine; and purple and green shadows from the mountain and forest lie on them; and these may be more lovely than the faint light of the winter noons of those latitudes, and the snowy pictures of frozen peaks which then show themselves on the surface; but before the day is half over, out come the stars—the glorious stars which shine like nothing that we have ever seen—and these, as they silently glide over from peak to peak of those rocky passes, are imaged on the waters so clearly that the fisherman, as he unmoors his boat for his evening task, feels as if he were about to shoot forth his boat into another heaven, and to cleave his way among the stars.

"Still as everything is to the eye, sometimes for a hundred miles along these deep sea-valleys, there is rarely silence. The ear is kept awake by a thousand voices. In the summer there are cataracts, leaping from ledge to ledge of the rocks; and there is the bleating of the kids that browse there, and the flap of the great eagle's wings, as it dashes abroad from its eyrie, and the cries of whole clouds of seabirds which inhabit the islets; and all these sounds are mingled and multiplied by the strong echoes, till they become a din as loud as that of a city.

"Even at night, when the flocks are in the fold, and the birds at roost, and the echoes themselves seem to be asleep, there is occasionally a sweet music heard, too soft for even the listening ear to catch by day. Every breath of summer wind that steals through the pine forests wakes this music as it goes. The stiff piny leaves of the fir and pine vibrate with the breeze like the strings of a musical instrument, so that every breath of the night-wind, in a Norwegian forest, wakens a myriad of tiny harps; and this gentle and mournful music may be heard in gushes the whole night through. This music, of course, ceases when each tree becomes laden with snow (which is the case for fully seven months of the year); but yet there is sound in the midst of the longest winter night.

"There is the rumble of some avalanche, as, after a drifting storm, a mass of snow too heavy to keep its place slides and tumbles from the mountain peak. There is also, now and then, a loud crack of the ice in the nearest glacier. Nor is this all. Wherever there is a nook between the rocks on shore, where a man may build a house, and clear a field or two—wherever there is a platform beside the cataract where the sawyer may plant his mill, and make a path from it to join some great road, there is a human habitation and the sounds that belong to it. Thence, in winter nights, come music and laughter, and the tread of dancers, and the hum of many voices. The Norwegians are a social and hospitable people, and they hold their gay meetings, in defiance of their Arctic climate, through every season of the year."[2]

To get from valley to valley during the long winter is not so difficult a matter as you would imagine. The ice makes a smooth road everywhere, on land and water alike, over which the snug sledges with their merry bells fly like the wind. These sledges are light little carriages, fitted with skates instead of wheels, that glide smoothly along the ice; they are drawn by horses, or by the

2   Miss Martineau.

SLEDGE.

swift-footed reindeer.

The people both of Norway and Sweden find pleasure in learning and in books, and they read a great deal; perhaps because the long winter nights give them much time within doors. In that part of Norway which lies to the north of the seventieth parallel, they never see the sun for two months at a time, but have a long dreary night; cheered, however, by beautiful lights in the sky, which are called the *Arora Borealis*, or the Northern Lights. To make up for this long winter night they have a summer day as long; a bright, hot two months, during which the sun is never out of sight. A traveller says, "It was eleven o'clock at night when we left the Laplanders (the strange little people who live quite to the north); and we reached the sea-side a few minutes before midnight. It was a glorious evening, the sun shining warm and ruddy across the calm sound. It was more like a sunset at Naples than what I had imagined of midnight within the Arctic circle."

This Scandinavian peninsula is a *long* country, with many varieties of climate between its northern and southern extremities. Look at the map, and you will see that much of Sweden lies between the same parallels as Scotland does; and, therefore, has somewhat the same climate. Fruit and corn are grown, and the people are busy farmers in what, compared with Norway, is almost a flat country.

Stockholm, the capital, is another Venice, built on many islands; it is nearly as beautiful as the fair Venice of the south, and is a very much cleaner, sweeter city. The people of this northern land are, now, a peaceable and industrious race; but the hardihood bred of sea and mountain led them in the old days to prefer a life of peril and glory on the wild seas to any wealth got by the tame crafts of the landsman. They held that whatever upon sea or land they were strong enough to take was fairly theirs. Wherefore these Norse Vikings became the terror of all lands bordering on the northern seas; and no country suffered more than England from their ravages. Indeed, they conquered much of the country, and settled upon the pleasant English lands they had subdued; so we may reckon the blood of the *Vikings* with that of the other races which go to make up the English nation.

LESSON XXVIII.
RUSSIA.

ONE half of Europe and a third of Asia, and that third larger than the whole of Europe, are included in the vast empire of Russia; indeed, it is a sort of giant among countries which looks large enough upon the map to swallow up the rest of the Old World. But with countries, as with people, good stuff is often wrapped in small parcels; and the greater part of Russia is not by any means "good stuff." A glance at the map will show you one or two reasons for this. There is a long sea-coast on the north, with a good many openings which might afford harbours for the ships. Yes, but it is the coast of a frozen sea; frozen rivers enter it—that is, the water enters under a coat of many feet of ice; frozen marshes border it; and the ground of Northern Russia, both in Europe and Asia, is frost-bound far below the surface to depths which the hot summer sun of these northern lands cannot penetrate. Siberia, as Russia in Asia is called, is more cruelly cold, more utterly desolate, than Russia in Europe in the same latitudes; thus Yakutsk is the coldest town in the world, though Archangel, on the White Sea, lies further to the north. But in the icy deserts beyond these places there are no towns; they are only frequented by hunters, who come hither for the seal, or to break the ice in quest of fish. Indeed, throughout the whole of Siberia, the population is not as much as one person to a whole square mile!

It is not only the northern plains which are excessively cold; the whole of Russia has a far colder, longer winter than you would expect from its latitude. The map will, again, tell you why: all through the wide empire there is not a mountain, hardly a hill, except the low chain of the Ural Mountains, which divide Russia in Europe from Siberia.

SEAL.

Suppose, for a moment, that we could alter the map: let us raise a great chain of Alps along the sixty-fifth parallel, a little to the north of Archangel. Have you ever taken shelter under a wall from a cold wind, or from the rain which the wind was driving before it? Our new Alps would act like such a wall, and would shelter the rest of Russia from the icy winds that blow down from the frozen plains and frozen seas about the pole.

Or suppose that, instead of raising new Alps, we only pile the Ural Mountains three times as high as they are at present—make them, in fact, as high as the Swiss Alps. What difference would that make? Do you not know the bitter winds that come to us in the spring, "Winds from the north-east, good for neither man nor beast"? Winds that crack our skins and blow the dust in our faces, and give us coughs and colds, and nip us up miserably? Perhaps you have wondered where these winds came from: look at the map and you will see—across the great plain of Europe, that is, over Holland and Northern Germany and Russia, over the Urals, which are not high enough to keep them out, straight off the frozen wilds of Siberia! No wonder these east winds should be so cold; no wonder, either, they should be so dry as to make our skins smart and crack; for until they reach the Baltic and North Seas, they pass over nothing but dry land.

Here is another reason why England has a climate so much pleasanter than that of the part of Russia in the same latitude. The sea does not get warm so readily as the land under the hot sun of summer, nor does it get so readily cooled in the winter. Therefore, people go to the seaside for cool breezes in summer; while, in the winter, the moist winds from the sea warm the land. Now, the sea hardly breaks into Russia at all; the north winds reach it over an ocean of ice; and the only other waters which border Russia are those of two or three inland seas. As you would expect, the part of Russia which lies, like England, between 50° and 55° north latitude, is a great deal colder than England in winter, and a great deal warmer in summer.

LESSON XXIX
RUSSIA.
PART II.

You will be surprised to hear that Russians who come to England for the winter complain that they cannot "stand the cold" of our country. The reason is that, while you might easily lose your nose by a bite from Jack Frost if you walked the streets of St. Petersburg in winter, the houses are kept far warmer than ours, by means of stoves and pipes, double windows and doors.

Even the peasants have enormous high stoves, taking up more than half of their single living and sleeping-room, and standing high in the middle of the floor. Do not suppose the space is wasted, however. The top of the stove is—the family bed! Up they all clamber, the men, oiled in their sheepskins, which never leave their backs night or day for a week. What dirty people! you say. Not so fast; they are clean once a week, at any rate, which is more than can be said for all English people. On Saturday afternoons you may see every soul in a Russian village, man, woman, and child, trotting off, towels in hand, to the public baths. There they go through a real boiling process; we should think ourselves killed if we had to endure the heat of these baths for ten minutes, but the Russians enjoy it, and strangely enough, they often rush straight out of these steaming baths, naked as they are, to roll in the cold snow outside.

You would suppose that Southern Russia, in the same latitude as France, and washed by the Caspian and Black seas, must be really pleasant. But here is a new kind of dreariness; all the way from the borders of Austria and Turkey on the west, to the limits of the Chinese Empire on the east, stretch the *steppes*. These are long, dreary, treeless levels, over which a man might ride day after day for months without ever coming to the end of them, and to-day he would see exactly what he saw yesterday and the day before—a wide, wide waste of pathless snow in the winter; an equally dreary waste of brown parched earth, upon which nothing grows, in the hot summer.

Notwithstanding all this dreariness in the north and south, Russia is a famous corn-growing country; she not only produces enough for the use of her own people, but is able to send many shiploads abroad, to England and other countries which have less room to grow corn for themselves. The middle of Russia is this fertile, corn-growing district; here, too, as well as in the north, there are immense forests, chiefly of pine, large enough in some cases to cover the whole of England. It is said that a squirrel might go from St. Petersburg to Moscow without ever touching the ground.

We have no space to describe the fine buildings of St. Petersburg, the capital city, which is so grand that it is called a "city of palaces"; and we must pass by the old, half-eastern city of Moscow, the ancient capital. Nor have we left ourselves room to speak of the long, slow rivers of Russia; not even of the great Volga, the largest river in Europe, which bears tea, carpets, slippers, pipes, silks and stuffs, and a thousand other things, to the great world's fair at Nijni Novgorod.

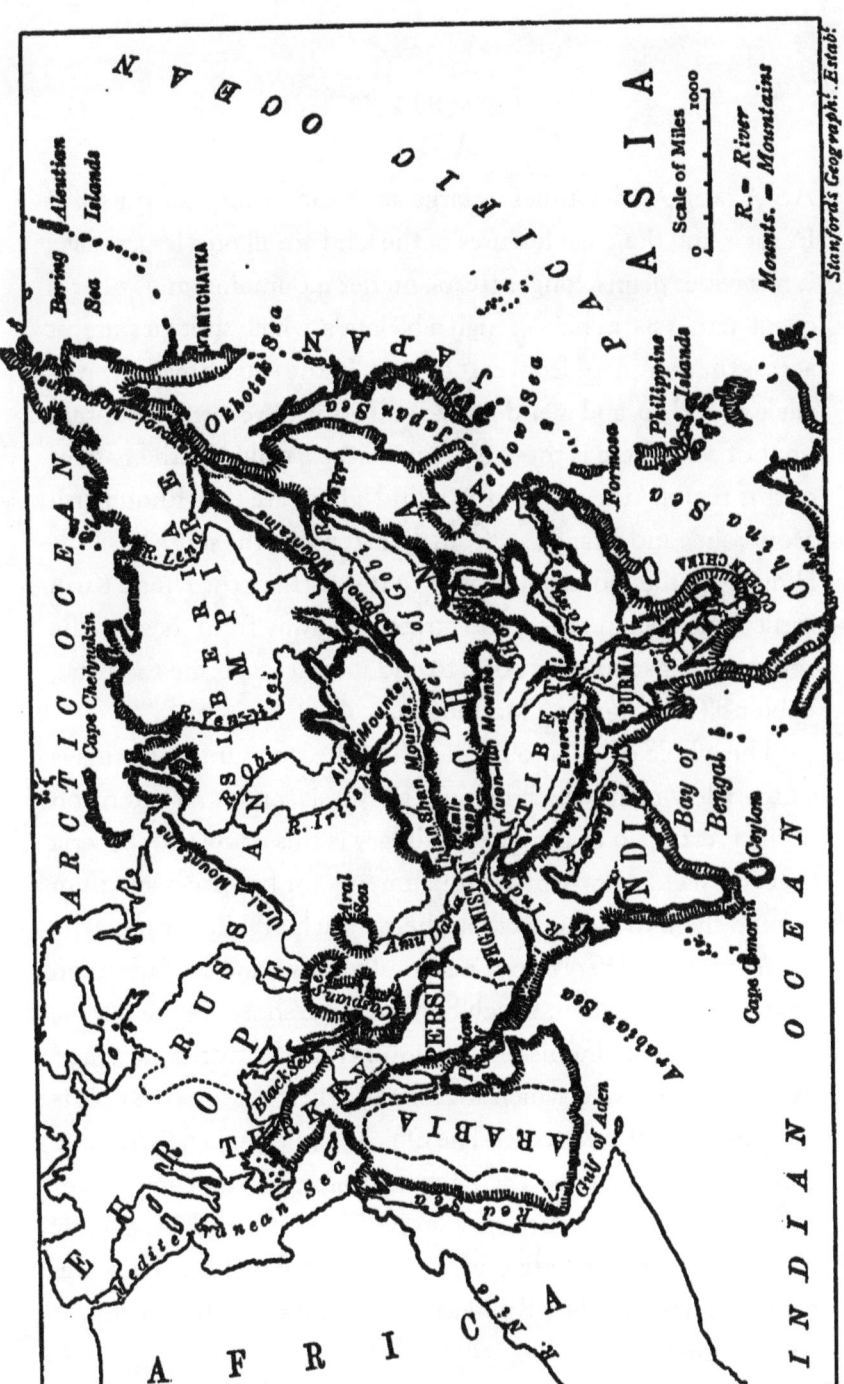

LESSON XXX.
ASIA.

ASIA is about five times as large as the adjoining continent of Europe, and the great features of the land are all on a larger scale; it has wider plains, longer rivers, higher mountains, and, what is peculiar to Asia, a chain of high tablelands, which stretches almost across the continent from east to west. In the square made by parallels 30 and 40, and meridians 70 and 80, is the central mountain knot of Asia; here is the lofty *Pamir Steppe*, called by the natives of this region "the roof of the world"; here are the Hindu Kush Mountains, and, branching from them towards the south-east, the Himalayas, the "abode of snow." To the north of the Hindu Kush is the Thian Shan range; and stretching away from these to the very north-east point of Asia, to end in East Cape, are the Altai, Yablonoi, and Stanovoi Mountains.

The whole of Asia to the north of these mountain chains is a dreary low plain which belongs to Russia, and is an extension of the great plain of Europe. So dreary is this country of Siberia that Russia has few worse punishments for her prisoners than to send them to live and labour here. Much of it lies beyond the Arctic circle, and here the ice never fully thaws; and the low frozen swamps called *tundras*, which lie round the shores of the Arctic, can hardly be distinguished in winter from the frozen waters of the ocean. The point which stretches furthest towards the pole is Cape Severo or Chelyuskin. The Obi, Yenisei, and Lena, the three great rivers which enter the Arctic, are slow and dull and dreary as the land they flow through; for several months in the year their waters creep into the sea under a deep coating of ice. They are, however, navigated by Russian steamers during the short, hot Arctic summer.

This Siberian plain is very important to Russia, not only because it is a hunting-ground where the sable and ermine, bear, wolf, and fox are hunted for their skins; it also possesses valuable mines, and gold is found in many of the rivers. The "fur country" is chiefly a broad belt of forest land in the west. The peninsula of Kamtschatka on the east contains several volcanoes.

On the west, the plain reaches to the south of the Caspian Sea, and this is a region almost as dreary as that round the Arctic. It is not frozen, but consists of sandy desert encrusted with salt and with many saltwater lakes; these are supposed to be the remains of a great sea which once covered the whole district. Into one of these lakes, called the Sea of Aral, two large rivers flow, the Amu Daria and the Syr Daria; and these and other rivers of this district never find their way into a sea connected with the ocean. Patches of brilliant green mark the spots where the rivers cross the desert, and these look all the more lovely in contrast with the barrenness around.

Washed by the Black Sea on the north, and by the Mediterranean on the west, is a country with many mountains enclosing beautiful valleys, where all our garden fruits grow wild, and where are great fields of roses grown to make "attar of roses." This country belongs to the Turks and is called Turkey in Asia; and along its Mediterranean coast is the Holy Land.

Its two great rivers, the Euphrates and the Tigris, flow nearly side by side over the plain of Mesopotamia, and join together before they enter the Persian Gulf. These rivers are famous in history, because upon the plain which they water stood Nineveh and Babylon, the two great cities of the ancient world.

LESSON XXXI.
ASIA.
PART II.

ASIA, like Europe, has three great peninsulas on the south. Arabia, the most eastern of these, has the Red Sea on one side and the Persian Gulf on another, and is a huge sandy peninsula without rivers. In the south is the Great Sandy Desert called *Dahna*, with here and there a green oasis sheltered by a few palm-trees marking the spot where springs of water bless the barren ground. Here the Bedouins wander, the wild shepherd Arabs who move their flocks from oasis to oasis in search of pasture, and who are the terror of travellers crossing the desert.

To the east of Arabia is Persia, which gives name to the Persian Gulf; this was once a mighty kingdom, though it is not of great importance now. The King, or Shah, visited England a few years ago, and his costly jewels were much admired; these eastern lands are generally rich in jewels. Much of the country is desert, but, where fertile, this also is a land of delicious fruits and fragrant roses. The people are civilised, and are skilled in some arts.

To the east of Persia, and lying partly between the 60th and 70th meridians, are the three rugged countries of Baluchistan, Afghanistan, and Turkistan, the people of which are chiefly occupied in rearing their flocks and herds. The sheep of Afghanistan have such broad fat tails that the shepherds make little cradles to support them; this country is also the home of the long-haired cats which we call Persian.

To the south-east of these is Hindostan or India—the central peninsula—a large rich country, crowded with people and towns, nearly the whole of which belongs to England. The greater part of Hindostan lies within the torrid zone; and here are elephants, lions,

TIGER.

and tigers, and other beautiful savage creatures of tropical lands.

The peninsula has mountain ranges on either side, and a tableland in the middle; its northern boundary is the great range of the Himalayas, containing the highest mountains in Asia.

Ascending the Himalayas, we are upon the wide, high tableland of Tibet, to the north of which, and separated from it by a mountain chain, is a great sandy desert called the *Gobi* or *Shamo*, both names meaning "sea of sand."

Both desert and tableland are subject to China, the country in the east, where most of the tea used in the world is grown. The two largest rivers, the Yang-tse-kiang and the Hoang-ho, fall into the Yellow Sea. This is the land of "fiddle-faddle shoes one scarcely sees;" the ladies have very tiny feet, and the gentlemen wear long hair plaited into *pigtails*. Mountain chains run across the country, and on the north you will see the *Great Wall* marked on the map; this is the longest wall which has ever been built, and it has been considered one of the wonders of the world. China and the countries subject to it form an empire. Hong Kong, a beautiful little island off the coast, belongs to Britain, and many British merchants live there.

The third southern peninsula ends in a curious long tongue which nearly reaches the equator; there are several countries in it, but the whole is known as Further India. The western provinces belong to England. Delicious sugar-candy is made in Cochin China, the country most to the east.

Japan, a kingdom made up of the islands beyond the Japan Sea, is another crowded and busy country of Asia. There are so many Japanese things in England, trays and boxes, and various ornaments, that most likely you are familiar with some of them. The people are fond of reading, and print many strange-looking books with odd pictures. Until quite lately, Europeans were not allowed to enter the kingdom, but now the Japanese are anxious to become as learned and as skilful as some of the nations of Europe and America; young Japanese have been sent abroad to learn, and foreign teachers are made welcome in Japan.

Not one of the nations of Asia is Christian, and the people are in many ways very unlike Europeans; they have generally yellow or brownish skins, and the men for the most part wear loose flowing clothes.

QUESTIONS ON THE MAP OF ASIA.

1. Name five seas on the east of Asia.
2. What sea is between the Japan islands and the continent?
3. What peninsula is on the north-east of Asia?
4. Name three great peninsulas on the south.
5. What empire occupies all the north of Asia?
6. What other great empire occupies the east?
7. Name four countries in the western half of the continent.
8. What sea, and what mountain chains divide Asia from Europe?
9. What ocean washes the south of Asia? The north? The east?
10. Name a cape upon each of these oceans.
11. What large bay divides the two great southern peninsulas? What island lies off the point of India?
12. What four countries form Further India, the most eastward of these peninsulas?
13. What waters are on the east and the west of Arabia? How is the Red Sea entered?
14. Which side of Asia has the most broken coast? Off which coast are there many islands?
15. Give the three names of the mountain range which stretches across the continent from the Pamir Steppe to the north-east point.
16. What great desert lies to the south of these mountains, and what mountains border the desert on the south?
17. To the south of this desert is a large country which is a high table-land. Name it, and say by what mountains it is bounded on the south.
18. How many great rivers rise in this table-land? Through what countries do they flow? Name three of them.
19. What great river rises in the Himalayas, and flows into the Bay of Bengal?
20. What river rises in the Pamir Steppe, and flows into the Sea of Aral?
21. The Euphrates and Tigris flow close together through Turkey in Asia. Into what waters do they fall?
22. What great river rises in the Altai mountains, and flows into the Arctic Ocean? Name its large tributary.
23. What two other great rivers flow into the Arctic?
24. Between what points would you measure the greatest length of Asia? About how long is it between these points?
25. Where would you measure the greatest breadth? About how broad is the continent there?
26. What parts of Asia are mountainous? What parts are plain?
27. Name the southern countries of Asia. The eastern? The central? The northern?
28. Name two great rivers of India; two great rivers of China; three of Siberia.

LESSON XXXII.
PERSIA.

Most people think of Persia as a land of nightingales and roses, of orchards and delightful flower-gardens; a land where peaches, plums, cherries, almonds—our choicest garden fruits—grow wild. It is true there are bowers of roses, and groves of fruit-trees, and banks of bright-coloured, fragrant plants in the mountain valleys, which are watered by hundreds of rills, and are sweet with the perfume of many flowers. And there are many of these valleys, for Persia is skirted by mountain ranges on every side but the east; generally, several of these ranges run in a line with one another, so that the mountain district often measures 200 miles across. There is a low, desert plain between the mountains and the Persian Gulf; and another low plain, very fertile, but unhealthy, between the mountains and the Caspian; and this is nearly all which lies outside of the mountains. Within this mountain girdle, what shall we find? We climb a steep ascent until we reach a *pass*, one of the fair and fertile valleys we have spoken of, where perhaps the land spreads out into a wide platform, and there are villages and orchards and pure streams. This pass only opens into another valley, and there is another and another mountain chain beyond; and we must make a long journey through several passes, some of them at a great height—several thousand feet above the sea-level—before we reach that which lies within the mountains. We shall be wise not to hasten our journey; let us linger in the delightful valleys, or among the black tents of the wandering shepherd tribes which we shall find on the mountain slopes. You think, perhaps, that Central Persia, so difficult to get at, surrounded thus by a bodyguard of mountains, should be indeed a garden of roses and all delights. Examine the map; you may see one or two straggling lines to mark waterways, which appear to end nowhere; but in all the great space enclosed by the mountains there is not a single river which reaches the sea; worse still, in the greater part of this district no rain ever falls. It is not surprising to see "Great Salt Desert" filling up the northeastern corner of the map; a land which is without water cannot fail to be desert. This dreary waste stretches over thousands of square miles, and is in some parts coated over with a layer of salt, which is often an inch thick; indeed, the whole of Persia, excepting on the borders of the Caspian Sea and among the mountains, is dry and barren, and is more or less a desert.

The coasts of the Gulf are burning sandy solitudes where little or no rain falls; and here the mountains bring no relief. These are awful mountains, high, hot, and barren, and the valleys between them are burning and barren, and rise like steps, six or seven of them, from the shores of the Persian Gulf to the tableland. For the last of the *passes* does not lead you into a valley; the mountains are but the sides of a high tableland which stretches into the lands that border Persia on the east, and is about as high as our highest English mountains.

The inhabitants of the tableland and of many of the mountain valleys are a wandering people called Iliyats, who dwell in tents and live by keeping cattle and sheep. In the cold winter months they and their cattle find food and shelter on the plains or in the valleys; in summer they seek the cool mountain pastures.

The true *Persians* live mostly in the cities, which are generally poor-looking, the houses being very mean, and the streets narrow and irregular. The bazaars, however, are well worth seeing; here are beautiful embroidered silks and delicate muslins, rich velvets, china, costly shawls, manufactured from the long wool of a certain goat, jewelry, perfumes, sabres—all made by the Persians, who are a skilful and ingenious people. Their rich, thick silks are very much admired; and the mulberry is largely grown in the north, to feed the silkworm. The Persians are a gay, lively race, fond of poetry and song, and extremely polite; but they are not considered sincere or truthful.

LESSON XXXIII.
ARABIA.

ALL round the coast of Arabia there is a strip of sandy desert, terribly hot and dry; backing this, on the Red Sea side, are high mountain chains with beautiful valleys, where there are streams and groves and orchards, and the precious date-palm; and where coffee is grown. Beyond the mountains there is desert in the north, desert in the south—a wilderness so awful that the Arabs themselves dare not venture into its horrid depths—sandy, burning desert everywhere, except for a mountainous district in the middle of the country, where many Arabs dwell.

Many tribes also dwell in the desert—even, it is said, in the terrible wilderness of the south. You need not pity them; *they* pity their brethren who dwell in the towns, and the inhabitants of lands where these burning solitudes do not exist, for they think no life so lordly, so happy, as the free life of the desert. How do they live? you ask. Here and there the desert yields some herbage; this is scanty enough, but by wandering from place to place according to the season, they do manage to find pasture for their flocks. In the *oases*—sunken, rocky valleys where there are springs and green herbage and date-palm—they may linger long; and these oases are frequent enough to make it possible for *caravans*, to cross the desert.

These are made up of persons who have business at the distant towns, and travel together for safety upon camels, which carry, also, food and water for the journey, and merchandise for sale. The *Bedouins*, the wandering Arabs of the desert, find these caravans profitable in more than one way: a company of them is hired to go with the caravan and protect it; or, on the other hand, they lie in wait to plunder the merchants, of whose coming they know beforehand.

Others besides the born sons of the desert find pleasure in this strange wilderness life; travellers say it is so unlike anything they have known before, that the hardships of a desert journey are made up for by the pleasure of novelty.

Mr. Warburton thus describes such an expedition:—"As long as you are journeying in the interior of the desert you have no particular point to make for as your resting-place. The endless sands yield nothing but small stunted shrubs; even these fail after the first two or three days, and from that time you pass through valleys dug out by the last week's storm, and the hills and the valleys are sand, sand, still sand, and only sand, and sand again. The earth is so samely, that you turn your eyes towards heaven; you look to the sun; he comes when you strike your tent in the early morning, and then, for the first hour of the day, as you move forward on your camel, he stands at your near side and makes you feel that the whole day's toil is before you. Then for a while, and a long while, you see him no more, for you are veiled and shrouded, and dare not look upon the greatness of his glory, but you know where he strides overhead by the touch of his flaming sword.

"No words are spoken, but your Arabs moan, your camels sigh, your skin glows, your shoulders ache, and for sights you see the pattern and the web of the silk that veils your eyes, and the glare of the outer light. Time labours on, and by-and-by the descending sun softly touches your right arm, and throws your lank shadow over the sand.

"Then begins your season of rest. The world about you is all our own, and there, where you will, you pitch your solitary tent; and there is no living thing to dispute your choice. When at last the spot had been fixed upon, and we came to a halt, one of the Arabs would touch the chest of my camel and utter at the same time a peculiar gurgling sound. The beast instantly understood and obeyed the sign, and slowly sank under me, till she brought her body to a level with the ground, then gladly enough I alighted. The rest of the camels were unloaded and turned loose to browse upon the shrubs of the desert, where shrubs there were: or where these failed, to wait for the small quantity of food that was allowed them out of our stores."

At its northern end the Red Sea forms two gulfs; between these two gulfs is a small peninsula, and in this peninsula is the *Wilderness of Sinai*, the desert in which the children of Israel wandered for forty years.

The Arabs are all Mahometans: Mahomet himself, the founder of this faith, was an Arab, born in the town of Mecca; wherefore this town, as also Medina, where the prophet was buried, are sacred spots which every Mussulman must visit at least once in his life. This leads to the *Haj*, the great yearly pilgrimage of Moslems from half over the world, from Africa, Turkey, Persia, India, Central Asia, who gather in huge caravans, and pitch thousands of tents outside the two sacred cities. The pilgrims take certain daily walks round the sacred mosque where once Mahomet sat and taught, make many prayers, drink often of the sacred well, and kiss the holy Black Stone. All these rites ended, they prepare to take their way home again through the weary deserts by which they came. Not all of them, however; many of the poorer sort, worn out with the hardships of the way, just drag themselves to the pavement of the great mosque to die where their prophet died; all day long, while the *Haj* lasts, men are engaged in burying these friendless pilgrims.

We must not quit Arabia without noticing ADEN, a very strong fortress on a barren, sandy spot, near the entrance of the Red Sea, which belongs to Great Britain. Steamers bound for India, which have come through the Suez Canal and the Red Sea, stop at Aden to take in fresh supplies of coal.

INDIA

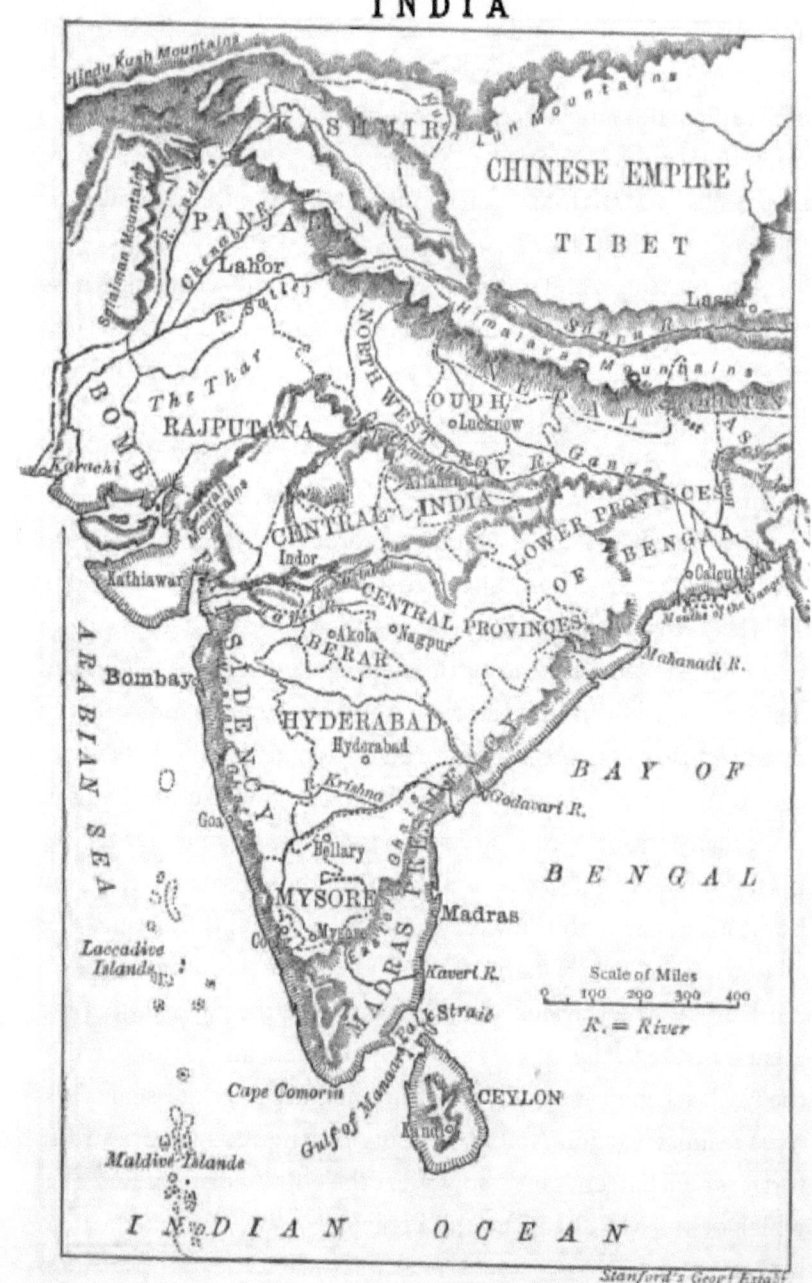

LESSON XXXIV.
OUR INDIAN EMPIRE.

WE all know a good deal about India: Indian shawls and Indian trinkets, work-boxes made of the scented sandalwood, and chess-men curiously carved in ivory; make us think of India as a land of rare and delicate products.

Probably we have seen some dusky-faced *ayah* (nurse), shivering in the graceful foreign dress she will not be persuaded to give up. She has come here with her nursling, some poor, pale, English baby, born under the hot sun of India, which has proved as trying to him as the frosts of England are to his Indian nurse. There are many English people in India, who are generally rich—judges and rulers of the people, officers in the army, and merchants—though there are also English soldiers and artisans. Most of the English residents try to escape to the hills before the hot season sets in; for then the heat is intense, and a huge fan, called a *punkah*, is kept constantly moving in every house.

You will see by the map that much of India is within the tropics; and, throughout the country, the year is divided, as in all tropical lands, into a *wet* and a *dry* season. The hot season begins about March; then the scorching rays of the sun destroy every green thing; there is never a cloud to deaden the glare unless it be a cloud of dust, which the hot dry wind has raised from the parched earth; everything you touch is hot-wood, iron, stone. At last, about the beginning of June, heavy clouds begin to roll across the sky, and then follows a thunder-storm, such as is never known in temperate regions; with much wind and torrents of rain.

When the thunder ceases, nothing is heard but the pouring of the rain, which comes down in a steady stream. The river channels soon overflow, and rushing streams add to the sound of waters everywhere. After several days the sky clears, and it would seem as if the parched earth had been covered with a magical mantle of green. The change is as great as if the bare brown fields of February in England were suddenly to burst into the green freshness of May. The rains continue to fall from time to time until September, when they depart amidst thunder and lightning as they came. This rainy season is called the wet *Monsoon*, a word which means "season." The period which follows the rains is the coolest and pleasantest time of the year. We have spoken of the great numbers of English people who live in India, not for pleasure, but because they have some kind of employment there. Perhaps you know the reason; this mighty country, as large as half of Europe, belongs to England! It is not quite right, however, to speak of India as a single country; it is a sort of continent in itself containing many nations, the people of which speak as many as thirty different languages. Our Queen has lately been declared *Empress* of India, as it was thought proper that the sovereign of so many states should be an empress. And a very splendid empire India is. "From the line of the Himalaya southward to the extreme cape on the Indian Ocean, India occupies a space more than *fifteen* times as large as our island of Britain; a journey across it from north to south, or from east to west (about 1800 miles), would require half a year if one travelled ten miles every day."

The story of how this great empire came to belong to England is too long to tell. India had long been known as a land where the merchants might load their ships with precious cargoes—gold and precious stones, silk embroidery, and ivory. In A.D. 1600, a company of London merchants got a charter from Queen Elizabeth, which gave them the sole right of trading in all seas east of the Cape of Good Hope. No trade was so profitable as that with India, and by and by these merchants gained permission from the native princes to build, here and there, warehouses for their goods, and fortresses to protect them. They formed these trading places at Surat, Madras, Calcutta, and Bombay.

For a hundred years or more, this company of merchants, called the "East India Company," carried on their trade, but did not gain much power.

The Emperors of India at that time were called the Great Moguls; they had many native princes under them who often rebelled, and the European settlers, French and English, were called upon to help one side or the other. The English merchants generally sent their soldiers to the aid of the Great Mogul. In the course of one quarrel, the Nabob Burajah Dowlah took the English town of Calcutta. The horrible crime of the "Black Hole of Calcutta" followed. One hundred and forty-six persons were shut up in a room twenty feet square. The air-holes were small. It was in the height of summer, when the fierce heat of Bengal can hardly be borne by natives of England, even when they dwell in lofty halls, and are cooled by the constant waving of fans, A night of agonies, too frightful to describe, followed. In the morning, only twenty-three wretched beings were drawn out alive from among the dead bodies of their comrades.

This event added, in the end, very much to the power of England in India.

In the following year, 1757, Colonel Clive, a great statesman and soldier, defeated Surajah Dowlah in the famous battle of Plassey, when 3000 men were victorious over 60,000 of the enemy.

This victory added the fertile country of Bengal, which now includes nearly the whole of Northern India, to the English.

At the present time, the East India Company has been done away with, and the Empress Victoria rules over India. She appoints a *Governor-General* to live in India and act for her there. The three great governments of British India are called Presidencies; these are, Bengal in the north, Madras in the east, and Bombay in the west. These cover the greater part of India. There is no longer a Great Mogul, but there are still many native princes, most of whom, however, are subject to the English Governor-General. There are two free states among the Northern mountains, Nepal and Bhotan; and France and Portugal have also a few scattered possessions. With these exceptions, India is under the rule of Great Britain.

LESSON XXXV.
OUR INDIAN EMPIRE.
PART II.

HINDOSTAN has on the north the lofty chain of the Himalaya Mountains, or rather, the vast tableland of Tibet, of which this range forms the southern border. Six of these mountains are fully five miles in height, and one of them, Mount Everest, is the highest mountain in the world (29,002 feet).

HIMALAYAS.

Are you trying to imagine how awful it most be to look up a mountain-wall five miles in height, high enough, you might think, to touch the sky? The Himalayas do not tower above the plain in this awful way, and nowhere do they look astonishingly high, because the snowy summits can only be seen from a great distance, which causes them to seem low. From the base of the mountains, only their slopes are to be seen, which are covered with various forest trees, and, higher up, with rhododendrons. A traveller who tries to cross this mighty ridge, which is three hundred and fifty miles in width, finds himself constantly shut in between the crags, and only now and then gets a glimpse of countless snowy peaks, and or wide glaciers.

In these high snowfields rise the three great rivers of India, the Indus, the Ganges, and the Bramahpootra, which water the low plain at the foot of the mountains. This low plain stretches right across the country, and the greater part of it is exceedingly rich and fertile.

The Ganges is the sacred river of the Hindoos, who make it part of their religion to bathe in its waters. For this purpose there are grand flights of steps leading down to the river from some of the towns; and upon these steps swarm crowds of the slight, dark-skinned Hindoos in their light cotton clothing. None are more crowded than the handsome steps at Benares, a sacred city in which there are more than a thousand idol-temples.

The melting of the mountain snows causes the rivers to overflow and flood the plain; and the rich mud they leave behind makes the fields fertile for the rice crops which support most of the people of India.

The towns and villages swarm with people, and most of these are engaged in tilling the soil; but they are not clever farmers by any means; their rude ploughs are drawn by oxen, and they reap their crops with the sickle. The soil, however, is very fertile, and yields cotton, sugar, delicious fruits, and several kinds of corn. The fields and gardens are full of scented flowers, and every village stands among groups of the shady mango-tree, which yields a refreshing fruit, and of the wonderful banyan.

This tree, which the Hindoos consider sacred, is a forest in itself; the branches produce long shoots which descend to the ground and penetrate the soil; so that in course of time a single tree becomes a vast green tent supported by many columns. No fewer than three hundred stems, each thicker than the trunk of a large oak, and more than three thousand smaller ones have been counted in a single tree. The fruit of the banyan is of a rich scarlet colour, and about the size of a cherry; it is eaten by the monkeys; and multitudes of these live, with birds and enormous bats, in the thick forest of its branches. An English child must think with terror of the dangers which surround an Indian village. There, the cry of the jackal would disturb his night, the fierce tiger might pounce upon him, some huge and deadly serpent, as the cobra, might wind about his body, or, if he ventured near the banks of the river, the jaws of the terrible crocodile might open to receive him. Nowhere are these dangers greater than in the district called

COBRA.

the *Sunderbunds*, which is the haunt of wild beasts. You will see by the map that the Ganges divides into many mouths before it reaches the sea, and the land between these, the *delta* of the river, is low and marshy and covered with jungle, that is, thickly matted, low-growing wood, where the beasts are safe, because men cannot easily penetrate. This district is called the *Sunderbunds*.

Very few of the mouths of the Ganges afford passage for ships, but upon the Hooghly, which is the most navigable, stands the great town of Calcutta, the "city of palaces," which is the most important town of British India. The "palaces" and grand houses and gardens belong only to that part of the city in which the English people live; the suburbs where the Hindoos swarm are very poor and mean. One of the strange sights of the city is the stately elephant marching through the streets with the *howdah* on his back, containing eight or ten persons; the driver sits perched upon his neck.

There are many other famous towns in this valley of the Ganges, which is the richest and most fertile part of India. Dacca, which stands where the mouths of the Brahmapootra join those of the Ganges, was once famous for its beautiful muslins, so soft and fine that they received the name of "flowing water." Patna gives its name to the best kind of Indian rice. Lucknow is famous for a terrible siege. Upon the Jumna, a tributary of the Ganges, are Agra and Delhi; the latter was celebrated once for its wonderful silks embroidered with gold. The natives of India are exceedingly clever with their fingers, and some of their manufactures are much more beautiful and perfect than English people can produce by means of machinery.

LESSON XXXVI.
OUR INDIAN EMPIRE.
PART III.

THE Indus drains the North-west of India. The northern part of its valley is a fertile district, watered by five rivers, all of which join the Indus; this district is called the Punjab, a name which means "five rivers." It affords pasture for vast herds of camels, cattle, sheep, and goats. Then follows a dreary tract, the Great Indian Desert, which is twice as large as Britan, and is covered with wave like ridges of sand, and can, for the most part, only be crossed by camels. On the coast there is a curious stretch of level land called the Runn of Kutch. This is a salt desert, which the sea overspreads during the wet monsoon.

Southern India, the peninsula, is occupied for the most part by a wide tableland called the Deccan, which is marked by waving treeless plains, flat-topped hills, and wide stretches of jungle. This tableland has, on either side, ranges of hills called Ghats or Ghauts. The Western Ghats are bold and rugged, and are covered with forests of teak, which affords a very hard kind of timber used in shipbuilding. Bombay, the capital of the Bombay Presidency, is the most important town on the western coast; it is a most unhealthy place for Europeans. The Eastern Ghats are much lower than the Western, and run at a greater distance from the sea. Between them and the Bay of Bengal is a low plain called the Carnatic, which would be very fertile but for the want of water. The Presidency of Madras lies along this coast, and the town of Madras is its capital. The Deccan has the Vindhya Hills on the north, and the Nilgiri Hills, upon which coffee is largely grown, on the south. Off the south point of India, and divided from it by Palk's Strait, is the delightful island of Ceylon, the "jewel of the eastern seas." So lovely is Ceylon that the Mahometans believe, here was the Paradise in which Adam and Eve dwelt. Upon Adam's Peak, the highest mountain in the island, is a mark like the print of a huge human foot; and the legend is that before he left this paradise, Adam climbed the mountain to take a last fond look, and that his footprint remained in the rock. Coffee plantations cover the lower slopes of the hills, and higher up are forests hung with beautiful creepers. The date-palm, cinnamon, spices, and sugar are among the rich products of this island where "every prospect pleases"; and there is a famous pearl-fishery off the coast. Ceylon, more than any other part of the world, abounds with precious stones. We must not leave India without a word about its gems; diamonds, rubies, sapphires, and emeralds are found in various parts. The most famous of Indian gems is the Koh-i-noor, the largest diamond in the world, which is now in the possession of our Queen.

A good deal of Further India, the curiously shaped peninsula to the east of the Bay of Bengal, belongs to England. BRITISH BURMA is the long strip of country along the north coast, containing the enormous delta of the Irrawadi. In this low country, cut up by many streams, are huge rice-fields; and the wooden huts of the people are raised high upon piles to save them from destruction by the river floods. Rangoon, the capital city, swarms with the gaily clothed, merry-looking natives. Further south, near the end of the peninsula, is MALACCA, a British settlement about as large as a small English county. Malacca exports tapioca and sago. SINGAPORE is a rich and pleasant island off the point which also belongs to Britain.

LESSON XXVII.
THE CELESTIAL EMPIRE.

PERHAPS China is, to us, the most interesting of eastern countries. Our cup of tea is a cup of fellowship with the natives of the "Flowery Land"; and we feel kindly towards the people who produce the precious plant, and who enjoy the infusion even more than we do. Then the Chinese are such queer folk, that is to say, their customs are so unlike our own, that we find information about themselves and their country very amusing.

We know that John Chinaman rejoices in a pigtail, made of his own hair or somebody else's, which reaches nearly to his ankles; that he begins to read or write at the bottom instead of at the top of the page, at the right-hand corner instead of at the left; that he likes the finger-nails of his left hand to be enormously long, in order to show that he does no hard work; and that, even when he is an old man; he finds much pleasure in flying a kite. Facts like these amuse us, but perhaps we do not know much about the appearance of the country, or the way in which the people live.

Besides China Proper, the Chinese Empire includes certain large and little known countries to the north and west. One of these is the Corea, the peninsula which partly shuts in the Yellow Sea; it has its own king, and only pays a small annual tribute in silver to the Emperor of China. It is supposed that there are no Christians in the country.

To the north of the Corea is Manchuria, whose people conquered China two centuries ago, and placed a Manchu sovereign at the head of the Celestial Empire. These three eastern countries, China, Corea, and Manchuria, are full of industrious people who dwell in houses, and either till the soil or gather together in busy trading towns.

Mongolia is an enormous country, which stretches westward as far as the Thian-shan Mountains. Here the people dwell neither in towns nor villages; they have no houses, and they do not till the land, but live in yurts, or tents, and wander about with their herds over the grassy lands at the foot of the mountains which shut in this tableland of Mongolia. A great part of this country is occupied by an enormous stony desert, called the Gobi or Shamo, which is 2000 miles in length and 500 in width; this desert is full of terror to the Chinese, who imagine it to be peopled with giants and dwarfs and evil goblins.

Tibet is, like Mongolia, a vast tableland; but while Mongolia is between 3000 and 4000 feet above the level of the sea (that is, the whole country is about as high as the highest of the British mountains), Tibet, which is about eight times as large as Great Britain, is raised on the average from 11,000 to 15,000 feet above the sea-level, that is, taken altogether, the whole region is as high as the highest peaks among the Alps. Here are bare grassy plains where herds of wild asses and antelopes feed, and the great long-legged wild sheep, whose horns are "so large that the fox is said to take up his abode in their hollows when detached and bleaching on the barren mountains of Tibet." Great lakes lie in these grassy plains; and, among the mountain snows, the famous rivers of India and China take their rise. The Tibetans are governed for the most part by their priests, who are called lamas, and live together in large monasteries, which are often rich and splendid; in one of these, which is famous for its gold-roofed temple, more than three thousand priests dwell. The people are, for the most part, wandering herdsmen, like those of Mongolia; they are only in very slight subjection to China.

Having noticed the countries which form part of the great Chinese Empire, we return to China itself,—a land which teems with people, containing more than 400 millions of inhabitants.

China consists of one long slope of more than a thousand miles, reaching from the Yun-ling or Snowy Mountains on the west, to the shores of the Pacific on the east. Mighty rivers drain this slope, the chief of them being the Yang-tse-kiang, 3000 miles in length, and the yellow Hoang-ho, both of which take their rise in the mountains of Tibet. These rivers bring down much earth in their course, and, when they overflow their banks, spread a rich coating of river mud over the low plains of the coast. In this way the Great Plain of China, which reaches from the city of Peking to the city of Nanking, has been made one of the most fertile regions in the world.

Not alone to natural causes does China owe the great fertility of its soil; there are no such diligent farmers in the world as the Chinese. They are not clever like the Scotch in inventing new plans, and in making use of machines; everything is done in China as it has been done for two thousand years; all farming work is done by hand, with no better implements than the spade and the hoe. Horses are never employed, because they eat too much, and there are so many people in China that every inch of ground is made use of to grow food for them; therefore, as there are no grass fields, there are but few of the creatures which generally live upon grass, such as horses, cows, and sheep.

Because they produce food for the people, farmers are held in high honour in China; only the learned men take higher rank, and these are quite the principal people, the noblemen or *mandarins* of the empire. The mulberry, rice, and the tea-plant yield the crops upon which the Chinese bestow the most labour; rice is the most important of these, because upon this crop the people mainly depend for food. Rice requires a great deal of moisture, so it is grown chiefly round the lower courses of the great rivers, and under the hot sun of Southern China.

The Chinese farmer is never at a loss for water to flood his *paddy* (or rice) fields, for canals are as common in the great plain of China as roads are in England; indeed, there are few good roads beyond the towns, and no railroads, as all the carrying and travelling are done by water. The Imperial Canal is one of the most famous public works of China; it connects the rivers Hoang-ho and Yang-tse-kiang, and is 700 miles in length. By means of this canal it is possible to go in a junk from Canton, the great southern port, to the royal city of Peking in the north, with only one interruption.

We are all familiar with the clumsy appearance of the Chinese junk, and perhaps we know the story of how a certain Chinese emperor, on being asked for a pattern for boats which should last for all time, took off his shoe, wherefore, upon that pattern all junks have been made ever since; but, though it is not a graceful object, the mandarin-junk offers a very pleasant and comfortable means of travelling.

CHINESE JUNK.

LESSON XXXVIII.
THE CELESTIAL EMPIRE.
PART II.

HONG-KONG, the Chinese for "sweet water," is a beautiful island; and the broad, well-kept, very clean streets of the town of Victoria show that the island is British, or at any rate, is not Chinese. The streets are everywhere planted with fine trees, which afford some shelter from the rays of the sun. The port is crowded with vessels of every shape and size, the most interesting of which are the junks; one end of these rises like a house, with windows and doors, two storeys above the water. All Chinese cities are very much alike; a rather shabby wall of blue bricks surrounds the whole; the houses are low, generally only one storey high, and never more than two; and the pagodas, or idol temples, which are sometimes as much as nine storeys high, tower above every other building, for it is not lawful in China to build houses as high as temples. The streets are narrow and not very clean, but are always lively, and filled with jostling crowds of good humoured Chinamen; how they manage to pass one another in their broad bamboo hats, the brims of which are often a yard across, is a marvel. The narrow streets are not, however, blocked up by wheeled carriages or carts; the coolies carry everything—timber, stone, iron, rice, whatever has to be moved; and they bear the rich people aloft on their shoulders in palanquins, or sedan chairs.

Coolie and mandarin alike have yellow complexions, narrow black eyes, small round noses, and plaited tails of hair; both wear long blue robes reaching nearly to their feet, but the coolie's blouse is of cotton, while the rich man wears dark blue silk, and his loosely-fitting silken trousers hang over black satin shoes with thick white soles, which are turned up at the toes like a boat. The lady's dress is very like her husband's, only that her robe is usually of pink or green silk, with wide flowing sleeves' lined with satin and splendidly embroidered; but the lady is rarely seen abroad, as her tiny cramped feet, called in China "golden lilies," are not of much use in walking.

AFRICA

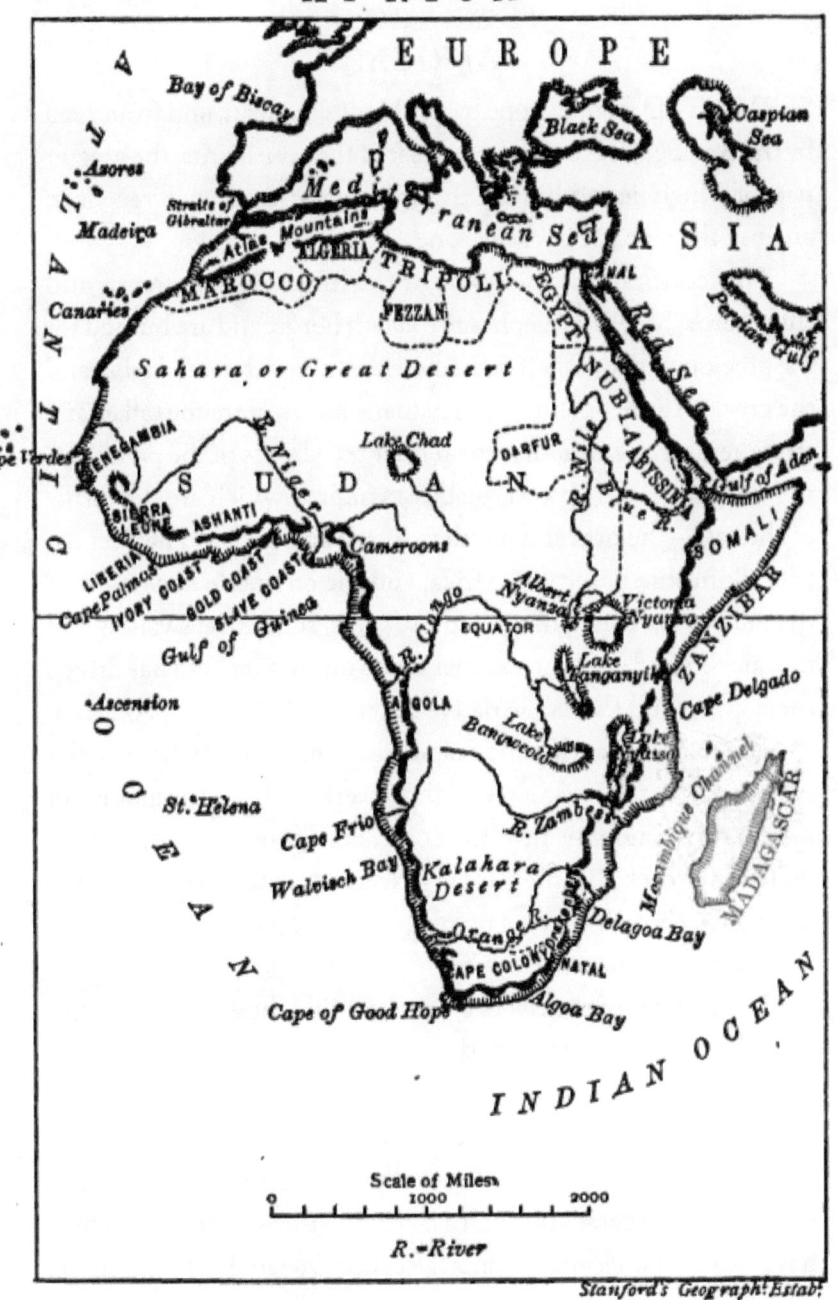

LESSON XXXIX,
AFRICA.

SEPARATED from Europe by the Mediterranean, and from Asia by the Red Sea, is Africa, the hottest of the continents, the greater part of which lies within the tropics, which, as you will recollect, enclose the *torrid* or burning zone.

This continent is the home of the huge hippopotamus and rhinoceros; here wild elephants roam in herds, and are hunted for the precious ivory of their tusks; here are the swift-footed zebra and the graceful antelope, and apes of many kinds. Here the tall giraffe stretches its neck to gather the tender top shoots of the palm; and in forest and desert prowl the beasts of prey which ate the terror of the rest—the lion and panther, jackal and hyena. The fleet ostrich skims the deserts of Africa, and the crocodile suns itself in the mud of its river banks. On these warm shores the swallow and the cuckoo find another summer when our winter cold has driven them away; and this is the native home of the African people.

The map shows that the sea nowhere finds it way far into the continent, that there are few mighty rivers, and that the mountain ranges run, generally, near the coast. For these reasons it is very difficult to reach the interior of Africa, and a great part of it is yet unknown, though there is no quarter of the globe that travellers have laboured more to explore.

The courses of the rivers generally guide these explorers; and many lives have been lost in the attempt to find the source of the Nile, the famous river in the east which flows into the Mediterranean. Bruce, the great traveller, discovered the source of the branch called the "Blue Nile," and other travellers have found that the White Nile passes through a lake upon the equator which they have named the *Victoria* Nyanza, after our Queen. Dr. Livingstone,

HIPPOPOTAMUS.

a brave missionary and explorer, was killed by the hardships and dangers he bad to endure while searching for the true source of the Nile. And great, indeed, are those dangers: in many places the explorers must make their way through marshes into which they sink shoulder deep, often having at the same time to hew paths for themselves through the thick growth of marsh plants. Hours of toil in such mud baths as these under a burning sun commonly end in fever, and this is often a fatal sickness. Then, too, there are the native tribes to be dreaded, so savage in parts of Africa that they eat the flesh of men; and even where the natives are friendly, the fearful wild beasts of forest and jungle are continually "seeking their meat."

Though so little is known of its beginning, no river is more famous in the history of the world than the Nile in its lower course. It was in this river that Pharaoh's daughter came to bathe when she found the infant Moses; and upon its banks is Egypt, the country of the Pharaohs, where Joseph stored the corn against times of famine. Corn grows freely in this land, because the Nile overflows its banks for many miles on either side every year, and leaves a thick bed of rich black mud for the corn seeds. No rain falls in the greater part of Egypt, and the river supplies the only water.

The fertile valley and delta of the Nile are shut in by burning deserts, and the fresh green of the springing corn looks all the more beautiful by contrast. Far and wide over the level delta in harvest time there wave fields of wheat and rice, sugarcane and cotton. In other parts are rich pastures dotted with herds of cattle, asses, sheep, and goats.

Cairo, the capital of Egypt, is the greatest city in all Africa. It contains an immense number of houses, with narrow crooked streets, over which the slim tapering minarets of hundreds of mosques rise like a forest. A crowd of people of all nations moves through its streets and bazaars. In 1869 the cutting of the Suez Ship-canal from the Mediterranean to the Red Sea was completed, and now about fifteen hundred great ships pass through this channel every year. Port Said, a modern town, stands at the Mediterranean entrance.

Going up the Nile from Cairo the first objects that attract attention are the great pyramids of Gizeh. These are huge buildings erected by the Pharaohs, the purpose of which it is difficult to discover; for enormous as they are, there is not room within them for a man to stand upright. It is supposed they were partly intended for royal tombs. They are broad at the base, and gradually taper to a point.

Nubia, which lies higher up the river, is included in Egypt; here the banks of the Nile are so high that the river never overflows, but the country is watered by regular rains. Nubia is famous for its fierce lions.

To the south of Nubia is Abyssinia, a fertile and pleasant country, which consists of a lofty tableland with many mountains and lakes, and valleys where the sugar-cane, cotton, coffee, corn, and various fruits grow freely. Abyssinia has a rainy season which lasts for several months. The people are of a brown colour, becoming almost white in the north; have curved noses and bright eyes, and are brave, active, and clever. They know how to make leather and to forge iron, and are acquainted with some other arts; but their chief wealth consists in their herds.

There are five states along the Mediterranean which are inhabited by two rather fair races,—the Arabs, who live in towns and occupy themselves in trading; and the Berbers, who live in tents and tend cattle. These are the States of Barbary; the lofty range of the Atlas Mountains runs through them; they have a pleasant climate, and the people are civilised. The name of Morocco, the western state, is known to us through the fine leather which is made all over the country; that and the red caps which take their name from the town of Fez are the only manufactures. Algiers, the adjoining state, is now a French colony, and has so delightful a climate that every year many invalids from Europe winter there.

LESSON XL.
AFRICA.
PART II.

SOUTH of the Barbary States, and stretching from the Atlantic on the one side to the valley of the Nile on the other, is the Sahara, or Great Desert. We are apt to think of the Sahara as a vast sea of burning sand over which the caravans journey day after day with never a cloud to screen them from the glare of the fiery sun overhead; where the hot wind of the desert drives the sand before it in terrible sand-storms, to settle at last in ridges or dunes, under which many a caravan, overtaken by these storms, lies buried. This is a true description of the northern borders of the desert, where these dunes form a great belt, 2000 miles in length and from 200 to 800 miles wide; but the interior consists in great part of tablelands. These are sometimes covered with sharp boulders of dark stone strewn so thick that the caravans can hardly make way; sometimes they are covered with small pebbles; and again, with a prickly plant which hurts the feet of the camels, though it affords them some food.

SAND-STORM.

It would not be possible to live in or even to cross this terrible desert, only that here and there are oases; these are tracts with springs of water, some coarse grass, and always the friendly shelter of the date-palm. There are hundreds of little oasis-states scattered throughout the desert where the few scattered inhabitants chiefly dwell. Some tribes of these earn a living by guarding the caravans in their passage across the desert; they are generally tall and handsome, and wear a shawl wound round face and head as a protection against the blown sands of the desert. The great caravan routes generally run from north to south, from the ports of the Mediterranean to the fertile countries of the Soudan. The merchants bring from the south ostrich feathers, gold-dust, slaves, and ivory; from the north they bring the cottons, trinkets, and cutlery of Europe.

South of the desert, between the 15th parallel and the 5th parallel north of the equator, lies Soudan. This is an exceedingly hot region: it is a vast tableland, with mountains, and many rivers and lakes which are fed by abundant rains. So in place of waterless desert with dried-up riverbeds as in the Sahara, the Soudan is full of well-peopled, fertile, and cultivated lands, with many settled nations and countries. This "land of the blacks" is merry enough of an evening, for the people of the villages turn out of their homes to sing and dance to noisy music. They do not play all day, however; they till their land, and know how to weave and dye cotton cloth made from cotton they have grown themselves; they live in towns, build two-storied houses, trade, and are a strong and civilised race. Only a small part of the Soudan is yet known to Europeans; it includes many countries, and some British and other foreign settlements on the coast.

Senegambia is the name given to Western Soudan, which is watered by the rivers Senegal and Gambia. France, Portugal, and

Britain have settlements here, those of Britain being chiefly on the river Gambia and on Bathurst, at its mouth. Sierra Leone, the "lion hill," three days' voyage south of the Gambia, forms part of the same colony: it was in the first place founded by English people as a refuge for slaves captured by our vessels along the coast; and to the present day English vessels watch the coast to prevent the export of slaves; but this does not affect this traffic in the interior, indeed one-half the inhabitants of the continent are the slaves of the other half. The trade of these British settlements is chiefly in palm-oil, from which the greater part of our soap is made at home.

Going south along the coast we come to the republic of Liberia, where the climate is dangerous to Europeans, though it suits the Liberians very well. Here, also, the oil-palm grows very freely, and its bunches of red and yellow fruit often have a thousand oil-yielding plums in each, the bunch weighing in some cases half a hundred-weight.

Passing by the Ivory Coast, we come to the GOLD COAST of Guinea, which is now entirely in the hands of the British. It is rich in the oil-palm, but the climate is exceedingly dangerous to Europeans. All attempts to introduce cattle and horses have failed, owing to the presence of the poisonous *tsetse fly*. The natives are negroes. The chief British station is Cape Coast Castle, named from its great church-like fort on the water's edge, beside the filthy native town.

Behind the Gold Coast lies the country of the warlike negro people called the Ashantees.

Adjoining Ashantee is Dahomey, a barbarous negro state where festivals are marked by the murder of many people, and where the king has an army of Amazons, or women-soldiers, to protect him.

The town of LAGOS, a little further on, belongs to Britain, and the steamers from Liverpool which trade with it carry home cargoes of palm-oil and cotton.

Next we reach the levels of the Niger district, a most unhealthy region of swamps overgrown with the deadly mangrove. This dark tree spreads over the low coasts of Western Africa as far south as the mouth of the Congo, that is, over the coasts of the district called Lower Guinea. It delights in mud, and its huge roots are constantly multiplying, and new roots are sent down from the branches, so that a single tree forms a dense grove in which the air is filled with unwholesome moisture fatal to Europeans. Little is known as yet of the inland countries of the Soudan. The black men native to Central Africa are marked generally by their black hair, protruding lips, and flattened noses; they are fond of ornament, and, above all, of dancing.

Of Eastern Africa, also, little is known as yet. The great eastern promontory is inhabited by a tall, well-made people, with brown skins.

South of the equator we come to a most interesting region which many travellers have, during the last forty years, tried to explore. These have discovered the two snowy mountains, Kenia and Kilimanjaro, the highest in Africa, the great lake Victoria Nyanza, through which the Nile flows, Tanganyika Lake, and Lakes Nyassa, Shirwa, and others. The great Zambesi river was explored by Livingstone. The east coast of Africa from Cape Delgado to Delagoa Bay is claimed by Portugal. The great island of Madagascar is not connected with Africa in any way; its people are distinct, and it has a government of its own.

LESSON XLI.
AFRICA.
PART III.

NEARLY the whole of South Africa belongs to Great Britain, which rules over all the land from Cape Frio on the west to Delagoa Bay and the Limpopo river on the east-with the exception of the small Orange Free State. Of these possessions, the CAPE COLONY is the most important; it includes all the land south of the Orange River; on the east it is bounded by the Drakenberg Mountains.

From the coast inwards, the country rises step by step in a series of terraces which run from east to west. These terraces sometimes rise into mountain ridges, whose seaward slopes are the most habitable parts of the colony, and are occupied by villages, corn farms, and vineyards, orchards and tobacco plantations. Beyond the Zwarte Bergen (Black Mountains) lie the wide undulating plains called the *Great Karroo*. Here farms are few, for water is scarce, and the water channels are dry except after thunder-storms; the land here is treeless—though in some parts stunted bushes are thinly scattered, and at most times of the year the prospect is dreary. Yet after rain, as if by enchantment, the whole plain is covered with a lovely green vegetation, with flowers of every hue. The heaths of the Cape Colony have a world-wide fame, as have the bulbous plants and orchids which cover the ground in September and October with a sheet of gaudy blossoms. The Great Karroo is divided into immense sheep "runs," whereon millions of sheep find pasture. Wool is the principal export of the colony.

The south-western peninsula, which ends in the famous Cape of Good Hope, is picturesque and beautiful with mountain and forest; it contains Table Mountain (3582 feet), whose flat top is often so covered with drooping clouds as to look like a table with a table-cloth on it.

The streams of the Cape Colony become furious torrents after rain, but almost disappear at other seasons. Not one of them is of much value for navigation; the largest, the Orange River, is obstructed by rapids and falls, and its mouth is blocked up by a sandbank. Cape Colony is not a hot country; it has four seasons as we have, though, of course, at opposite times—January falling in midsummer, July in midwinter. Thorns and prickles are characteristic of many South African plants; some trees, such as the "dornboom," have spikes which have been compared to ox-horns; and there are many odd-looking cactus-like plants. Wheat is largely cultivated, and so are maize, oats, and barley. The grapes of Constantia, on the peninsula of the Cape of Good Hope, are said to be the finest in the world.

Since the lion, leopard, and other beasts of prey have been driven away to the north of the Orange river, the sheep have increased in an extraordinary degree, and they yield an immense quantity of wool. Oxen dragging great canvas-covered waggons are the chief means of conveyance in the colony, except where railways have been constructed. In the ostrich farms here the birds are fenced in and stabled like sheep or horses, to be plucked of their valuable feathers when these come to maturity; their eggs are batched in artificial nests warmed by hot water.

There are not many people as yet in the colony, only about four or five to the square mile: the Europeans—British and Dutch—are the most numerous. Besides these, there are a few Hottentots left, who are light-hearted, short, and of a pale yellow-brown colour; and the Kafirs, who are tall, dark brown in colour, active, and well made. The Hottentots were the only inhabitants when the colony was discovered.

The capital is Cape Town, a large town which lies between Table Mountain and the shores of Table Bay; gas-lighting, gardens, tramways and railway stations give it all the air of a European town. Port Elizabeth, on Algoa Bay, is the second town, and is a bustling seaport full of warehouses and stores to which huge waggons bring down the wool and hides of the interior for shipment. Grahamstown is an important place in the interior.

KAFIRLAND is the fertile and well-watered country which lies between the Drakenberg Mountains and the Indian Ocean; it is inhabited chiefly by Kafirs, but is under the control of British magistrates. NATAL, to the north of Kafirland, also lies between the Drakenberg Mountains and the Indian Ocean: it is full of mountain spurs, which slope down from the Drakenberg; it has a delightful climate and a fertile soil; cattle and sheep are reared on the wide grass pastures, and corn crops, coffee, and sugar are largely grown. The natives are Kafirs, although Hindoo coolies are imported to do the work.

There are but few Europeans—English, Dutch, and German, and these live for the most part in the two towns of the colony, the seaport of Durban or Port Natal, and Pietermaritzburg, where the British Governor lives.

The Orange Free State is a republic, and consists of grassy plains upon which many sheep and cattle are fed, so that sheep-farming is the principal business of the Dutch settlers. The Transvaal lies between the rivers Vaal and Limpopo; vast herds of cattle and flocks of sheep are reared on the hills, and the Boers, or Dutch farmers, are the principal colonists, but the greater part or the inhabitants are the native Kafirs.[3]

We have no room to speak or the various Kafir kingdoms in the interior of South Africa, nor of the islands off the coast, not even of the small British island of ST. HELENA.

---

3 From the article on AFRICA in 'The London Geography,' by Keith Johnston, F.R.G.S.

QUESTIONS ON THE MAP OF AFRICA.

1. What sea divides Africa from Europe?
2. Name four African countries which have coasts upon this sea.
3. A range of mountains on the north-west coast which crosses two of these countries?
4. Name the great desert which lies at the south of these northern countries.
5. What large river flows into the Gulf of Guinea?
6. How are various parts of the Guinea coast named?
7. Name three States in the south part of this western shoulder of Africa.
8. What general name is given to the lands south of the Sahara?
9. Name a lake in Sudan.
10. Name a great western river below Sudan which appears to begin in a distant lake.
11. Name five large lakes in the eastern half of the continent.
12. What large river flows into the Mozambique Channel, to the south of these lakes?
13. What great northward-flowing river appears to begin in the Victoria Nyanza Lake?
14. Through what countries does this river flow? What sea washes their eastern coast? What country in Asia ia on the farther aide of this sea?
15. What tributary of the Nile begins in the mountains of Abyssinia?
16. What country, watered by the Nile, has coasts upon two seas?
17. How is the Red Sea connected with the Mediterranean?
18. By what gulf must vessels leave the Red Sea?
19. What large country lies to the south of this gulf?
20. What is the eastern coast of Africa called? Name a cape on this coast; two bays; a large island in the Indian Ocean.
21. Name half-a-dozen African islands, or groups of islands in the Atlantic.
22. Any capes or bays on the western coast.
23. At what point do Africa and Europe nearly join? What strait separates them?
24. Name a large desert in Southern Africa south of the Zambezi.
25. What country occupies the southern point of Africa? A smaller country to the north-east of this?
26. What river bounds Cape Colony on the north?
27. What mountain range runs near the east coast of this south end of Africa?
28. What famous cape is at the south-west corner?
29. How do the mountains of Africa lie, in the interior, or near the coast?
30. State roughly the length and breadth of Africa at the longest and broadest parts.

LESSON XLII.
THE NEW WORLD.

THE three continents which we have spoken of are known as the *Old World*. When this Old World was already very old, when men had lived in it for fifteen centuries believing it to be the whole of our habitable earth, a great joy was granted to a faithful man. To this man, Christopher Columbus by name, it was given to discover a new world—a new continent really, but so vast, so beautiful, so filled with all manner of riches, and so unlike the world they already knew, that men loved to speak of it as the *New World*.

Columbus, who was a native of Genoa in Italy, and whose business it was to make maps and charts, became convinced that the earth was a sphere. That being so, he thought that if after leaving the Mediterranean he continued to sail to the west, he must at last come to China, unless there were some, undiscovered land between.

He thought of this night and day, and laid his plans with great care; but, alas! he was a poor man, and ships, money, and men were wanted before he could work out these bold projects. He could get no help in his own country, so he went to Spain, and after much entreaty Isabella, the queen, granted him three ships, to do what it was thought had never been done before, to sail right across the perilous ocean without knowing what he should come to.

His men grew mutinous, for they had to face many terrors on the way; but Columbus kept up heart and hope, and after many a weary watch land was at last sighted; land that no man from the Old World had ever gazed upon. "We praise Thee, o God," rang out from them all, but they little knew, and Columbus himself never knew, for how much they were praising God; they little dreamed how vast were the continents of the western hemisphere which they had lighted upon.

Wild were the rejoicings in Spain, and great was the honour with which Columbus was received; and very memorable has he made that year of our Lord, fourteen hundred and ninety-two.

Many followed where Columbus had led the way; other nations of Europe sent men to explore this wondrous new world, and they returned full of its marvels. Perhaps at every fireside of our own Britain strange tales, better than fairy lore, were told of these lands of the west—of their mighty rivers, so wide and full that they looked like great seas rolling into the ocean; of forests bigger than any known country, those trees were gay with flaming flowers; of the tiny humming-bird, like a sparkling jewel, hiding itself in these huge blossoms; of other birds of gorgeous plumage, the parrot and toucan; of the huge condor, the largest of all flying birds.

Fearsome tales, too, of the alligator in the great rivers, the boa-constrictor, and the rattlesnake. Tales of strange beasts which carry their young in natural bags or pouches; of marvellous monkeys, which make use of their tails by which to swing themselves from tree to tree. But they told of no beasts so large, nor indeed so handsome, as those of the Old World.

Tales were told, too, of rich cities with splendid palaces and many gold and silver ornaments; of the gentle, kindly people of these cities, who welcomed the strangers lovingly, made feasts for them, and gave them rich presents. And then came dark tales of how these gentle people were cruelly slain, and their riches and cities taken by their strange guests. Englishmen were glad then, and are glad now, that this shameful deed was not done by countrymen of theirs.

The continents came to be called America, North and South, after a man who sailed with Columbus, and who wrote a book about what he had seen.

By degrees people came not only to see but to settle. Many Portuguese and Spaniards settled in South America, and in that part of North America which is about the Gulf of Mexico, one of the two countries where the people were so treacherously dealt with.

The French and the Dutch came to North America; and, by-and-by, the English, in such number that now an English-speaking people fills nearly the whole of North America excepting Mexico, the part settled at first by Spain. What became of the native people? There were not a great many of them, and only in two countries did they dwell much in cities. Most of them lived by hunting; and there was room enough for the them as well as for the white settlers. They are generally well-made people, with reddish-brown skins, straight features, and straight hair, and they have very keen sight and scent. They do not like work, and do not like to live in cities; therefore they do not readily become civilised, and are gradually dying off. Those at the south point of South America are perhaps the tallest people in the world, while the aborigines on the Arctic shores, a different race, are very short and fat, and live chiefly upon fish.

NORTH AMERICA

LESSON XLIII.
NORTH AMERICA.

The Great Western Continent reaches nearly from pole to pole, a length of 9000 miles; it is four times as large as Europe, and is second only to Asia, which is the largest of the continents. The longest range of lofty mountains in the world runs through the two Americas, passing through the isthmus which joins them. Throughout its length this range keeps near the Pacific coast, thus giving a long slope towards the Atlantic, down which flow the mightiest rivers in the world. In North America the principal range is known as the Rocky Mountains. Mount Hooker, the highest summit (16,760 feet), is in the north; but nearly in the centre of the range are twenty-five peaks, all of which are as high as the loftiest summits of the Alps. On the coast is another great mountain chain, the Coast Range of the Pacific; Mount St. Elias (14,970 feet), which is a huge volcano, and Mount Fairweather, both in the north and near the coast, are the two highest points. Between these two long mountain ranges are high tablelands.

Central America is filled with high tablelands, from which many volcanic cones rise; of these Popocatepetl (17,784 feet) and the Peak of Orizaba (17,879 feet), on the Mexican tableland, are the highest summits of North America. Great lowlands fill the centre of North America, reaching from the Arctic shores to the Gulf of Mexico. Towards the eastern coast the continent again rises into the rather low Alleghany Mountains.

The great island of Greenland, lying to the northeast of the mainland of America, is about eight times the size of Great Britain, and is covered with one vast field of ice, which reaches from sea to sea. Some Eskimos and a few Danish settlers make their homes here for the sake of the sealskins and whale oil with which they trade.

From the Arctic shores to about the fiftieth parallel a wide and dreary British territory stretches, which is known as the DOMINION OF CANADA; part of the southern boundary of this territory is formed by the river St. Lawrence and its chain of mighty lakes.

South of the lakes, and reaching to the northern shore of the Gulf of Mexico, and right across the continent from ocean to ocean, we find the United States of North America, a very great country, rich and powerful, with many towns and people. These people speak the English language, and the country once belonged to Britain, but now it is a Republic, formed of many States united under one government. New York, Boston, Philadelphia, Washington, St. Louis, and New Orleans are some of the principal towns.

The climate in the Southern States is warm, and much rice, sugar, and cotton are grown; a great deal of the cotton grown here is made into calico in the English factories. There is a sad history connected with the cotton and sugar plantations; white people are not able to do the necessary field work under the hot sun of these States, so for many years it was the custom to bring shiploads of people from Africa, and set them to work in the fields as slaves. These poor slaves were often cruelly used; they were beaten with thongs to make them work, and children were sold away from their mothers, and wives from their husbands. But now, happily, there are no longer slaves in America; a great war recently put an end to so sad a state of things; the blacks still do the work, but they are free, and work for wages like other labourers.

Through the low central plain of North America flows the mighty Mississippi, the "Father of Waters," with its tributary the Missouri, as great as itself; it receives many other large tributaries, and only one other river in the world bears such a flood of water to the ocean.

On either side of the Mississippi stretch the wide, rolling *prairies*, or meadows, of North America. They are very level, and are covered with tall grass and brilliant wild-flowers, but are without trees. When cultivated, these prairies yield corn crops in the Northern States, and rice, cotton, sugar, oranges, and other products of warm lands in the States to the south.

To the south of the United States is Mexico, which lies almost entirely upon a high tableland, and therefore has a pleasant climate, though it is in such warm latitudes. It has huge volcanoes, and mountains rich in silver and gold. The capital city is Mexico, which has a fine cathedral, and as many as eighty churches. This is one of the countries where the Spaniards found cities and wealth, of which they robbed the gentle and civilised people.

Central America, the curiously shaped narrow part between the two continents, is also a tableland; and through the narrow neck of Panama a low range of hills runs, to rise presently into mighty, snow-capped mountains, many of them volcanoes. There are works on foot for making a canal through the isthmus of Panama, thus to connect the two oceans.

One little bit of Central America belongs to Britain, namely, BRITISH HONDURAS, or Belize, on the Gulf of Honduras; it is valuable for the mahogany and logwood of its forests, which are floated down by the rivers to the sea and shipped in large quantities.

THE WEST INDIES

THE West India Islands form a long archipelago (or sea of islands), that reaches in a curve from between Florida and Yucatan round to the coast of South America. The Spanish island of Cuba is the largest and most important of these; Hayti, where there is a negro republic, and Puerto Rico, also a Spanish island, and JAMAICA, a British island, are the next in importance of the West Indies.

Jamaica has two or three large towns, and exports rum, molasses, allspice, coffee, dye-woods, and mahogany. TRINIDAD, where there are pitch lakes, BARBADOS, ANTIGUA, and DOMINICA are also rather important islands belonging to the British. The BERMUDAS and BAHAMAS also belong to Britain; each of these groups consists of several hundreds of low-lying coral islands, but only a few are inhabited; most of them are mere coral reefs and rocks.

Though almost all the islands lie within the torrid zone, the climate of the West Indies is made pleasantly cool by the surrounding seas. The northern islands have a rainy season during the summer months; Jamaica and the southern isles have two rainy seasons. Yellow fever is the scourge of the coasts of the islands during the rain, and they are exposed to fearful hurricanes. The warm climate and the plentiful rains make the West Indies well suited to the growth of sugar-cane, tobacco, and tropical fruits. Sugar, rum, and molasses; cotton, coffee, and cacao; indigo and dyes; spices, oranges, bananas, pineapples and many other fruits, are exported.

LESSON XLIV.
THE DOMINION OF CANADA.

THE wide "Dominion of Canada," which belongs to the British Crown, stretches across the continent of North America, from ocean to ocean, and from the United States on the south to the shores of the Arctic. The north-west corner, the peninsula of Alaska, belongs to the United States; the icy and desolate peninsula of Greenland belongs to Denmark; the rest of the continent north of the 49th parallel is under British role.

Nowhere will you find a straighter boundary line than that between the "Dominion" and the western United States. For several hundred miles a cutting thirty feet wide is made through the forests, and an iron pillar, standing four feet from the ground and painted white, is placed at the end of every mile. The mighty chain of lakes, whose waters are carried away by the river St. Lawrence, forms part of the southern boundary. Lake Superior is the largest fresh-water lake in the world; and Michigan, Huron, Erie, and Ontario are all so large that they are like inland seas, and, like the sea, are subject to storms so violent that great waves like ocean breakers dash against the shores.

All the important towns of the Dominion lie either on the shores of the lakes or on the lower course of the river, for this chain of lakes united by rivers forms the highway by which trade with the forest lands of the north and west is carried on.

The boats used in this traffic are exceedingly light, because, in the course of a voyage westward, it is often necessary to carry both boat and cargo over a *portage*, the name given to the land passage across which everything most be *carried*.

It is necessary for the *voyageurs* thus to carry their boats, because there are many rapids and waterfalls in this great waterway. Perhaps a river arrives in its course at a lake which lies much lower than itself. Its waters must needs enter the lake, so down they pour in a great waterfall, it may be, a hundred feet deep.

When the *voyageurs* approach these dangerous cataracts they draw their boats to land, and carry them over a portage, until smooth waters are reached.

The most famous waterfalls in the world are in the river Niagara, which connects Lakes Erie and Ontario. The deep booming sound of the waters may be heard at a distance of two or three miles. We say falls, because there are two, divided by Goat Island, which rises in the midst of the foaming river. That on the Canadian side of the river is called the Horseshoe Fall on account of its shape, and is considered the more beautiful of the two.

THE NIAGARA

During the bright, hot Canadian summer, rivers and lakes are lively with the beat of many oars and with the songs of the boatmen, whose "voices keep tone as their oars keep time." Sometimes the boats go in companies called brigades, which look gay enough as they start on their voyage, hundreds of miles long, to some distant western station, from which they will bring back boat-loads of furs to be shipped to Europe. All this ends when winter sets in.

For five months in the year the river above the town of Quebec is frozen, and the sleigh with its merry bells is then the usual means of travelling.

The moment the snow falls, wheeled carriages and carts give place to sleighs. "These beautiful vehicles are mounted on runners, or large skates, and slide very smoothly and easily over the snow. They are usually drawn by one horse, the harness and trappings of which are covered with small round bells, which make a very pleasing, cheerful, tinkling music on the Canadian roads."[4]

Indeed, winter is a joyous time amongst the Canadians. The cold is intense, but the air is clear, the sun is bright, the roads are crisp, and every one who can wraps up in fur and turns out for a merry sleigh ride. Here is a description of a Canadian scene in winter: "From the hill on which we stood, the whole valley, of many miles in extent, was visible. It was perfectly level, and covered from end to end with thousands of little hamlets and several churches, with here and there a few small patches of forest. Several small vessels lay embedded in ice at the month of the river, beyond which rolled the dark, ice-laden waves of the Gulf of St. Lawrence. The whole valley teemed with human life. Hundreds of Canadians in their graceful sleighs flew over the roads, and the air was filled with the faint sound of tinkling bells."[4]

Such a scene as this could only belong to Canada Proper, that is, to the two provinces of Quebec and Ontario. Quebec lies on the lower course of the river St. Lawrence, and Ontario higher up, on the northern shores of the lakes. These provinces were, until lately, called Upper and Lower Canada, and they are almost the only part of the wide "Dominion" where there are towns and many people. This part of America was visited, in the first place, by a French voyager named Jacques Cartier, who found the country peopled by Indians

---

[4] 'Hudson Bay.' R. M. Ballantyne

who were friendly and kind to the strangers. Here and there were groups of wigwams—Indian huts—and these the Indians called *Kanata*, which means village, or place of huts; but the Frenchmen took this word for the name of the country, which has ever since been called Canada. Shortly after, other Frenchmen came, who took the country from the kindly Indians and settled themselves in the part now known as Quebec. These French settlers built Montreal, Niagara, and other towns; and, on the top of the Heights of Abraham, which are steep as a wall towards the river, they built the strong town of Quebec. This they defended with many guns placed on the hill slopes, and in the walls and forts, until Quebec became almost as strong and as difficult to attack as the fortress of Gibraltar. But war broke out between England and France, and an English army was sent, under the command of the young General Wolfe, to attack Quebec. He did not attempt to lead his men up the heights under the French guns by daylight, but chose a dark night for the attack. Then, with muffled oars, the English rowed silently past the town, landed higher up the river, climbed up to Quebec from behind, and were in the enemy's camp before the alarm had been raised. The French were brave, and a fierce battle followed, in which General Wolfe fell—not, however, before he knew that the French were defeated, and that Quebec was in the hands of his men; then he said, "I die content."

Since this victory (1763) Canada has remained in the hands of the English. The people of the province of Quebec are descended, for the most part, from the early French settlers. They are called *habitans*, and are a gay and warm-hearted people, who dislike changes, and care only to live as did their fathers before them. Most of them are farmers, and their farms are long and narrow, so that the farm buildings lie on the bank of the St. Lawrence, and the fields stretch away far to the north. In the summer many of the men are employed as voyageurs, that is, they row the boats engaged in the fur trade. Quebec and Montreal are the chief towns. Montreal is a large and handsome city, with fine shops, baths, hotels, and public buildings. Quebec is beautifully placed; it consists of a lower and upper town, and round the upper town are walls and fortifications. The streets are narrow and even steeper than those of Edinburgh, and the houses are high. The best shops and some of the houses of the rich people are in the upper town.

Ontario, formerly Upper Canada, is more fertile than Quebec, and is chiefly peopled by English settlers, many of whom are farmers, as in the province of Quebec. The towns are new for the most part, and the streets are broad and straight and rather stiff-looking. The chief town of the province is Toronto, a large and busy city, with long streets, many shops, and busy wharves. It is one of the wonders of the West, because, unlike the slow-growing cities of the Old World, it has reached its present importance within a century. Ottawa is also an important town, because it is now the seat of Government for the Dominion of Canada.

LESSON XLV.
THE DOMINION OF CANADA.
PART II.

NEW BRUNSWICK—where there are forests of huge pine, and where the cutting of timber and the building of ships are the chief occupations—and NOVA SCOTIA are also included in the Dominion. Fishing is the principal business of the latter province, and great quantities of dried fish are sent to the Mediterranean.

The NORTH-WEST TERRITORY is the name now given to nearly all the rest of British North America. This country used to be called the Hudson Bay Company Territory. Hendrick Hudson discovered the bay from which this vast tract was named. He hoped to carry his discoveries further, but his crew mutinied, and put him into a little boat, together with eight sick seamen, provided only with a little meal, a musket, and an iron pot; and then they left him to perish in the bay named after himself. In the year 1669 a company was formed in London for the purpose of carrying on the fur trade in the regions round Hudson Bay. This company had the sole right of trading in all the country watered by rivers flowing into this bay, and of building *forts* here and there for the protection of their trade. This vast tract is now part of the Dominion, but the fur trade is carried on as before.

"Imagine an immense extent of country many hundred miles broad and many hundred miles long, covered with dense forests, great lakes, broad rivers, wide prairies, swamps, and mighty mountains, where the axe of civilised man has never been, and where roving hordes of Red Indians and myriads of wild animals are the only tenants. Imagine, amid this wilderness, a number of small squares, each enclosing half a dozen wooden houses and about a dozen men, and between each of these establishments a space of forest varying from fifty to three hundred miles in length, and you will have a pretty correct idea of the Hudson Bay Company's Territories, and of the number of and distance between their forts."

The name of *fort* is given to all these stations, though very few of them are fortified.

The most valuable of the furs taken in this region is that of the *Black Fox*, and badger skins, beaver skins, deer, bear, wolf, otter, and seal skins, as well as whale oil, dried and salted fish, feathers and quills, are among the stock the Indians bring to the forts for sale.

The natives visit the forts of the white men twice a year—once in October, when they bring in the produce of their autumn hunts; and again in March, when they come in with that of the great winter hunt. After the furs are collected in spring at all the different outposts, they are packed in bales and sent by means of boats and canoes to the three chief depots on the sea-coast, namely, Fort Vancouver, at the mouth of the Columbia River, on the shores of the Pacific; York Fort, on the shores of Hudson Bay; and Moose Factory, on the shores of James Bay, whence the bales are sent in the Company's ships to England. The whole country in summer is lively with the passing of brigades of boats laden with furs; the still waters of the lakes and rivers are rippled by the paddle and the oar; and the echoes are awakened by the merry voice and tuneful song of the hardy *voyageur*."[5]

The aborigines (that is, the native inhabitants) of North America belong to the race of people known as Red Indians. They consist of a great number of nations or tribes, some of which bear a bitter hatred to certain other tribes. Among these nations are the Crees, Stone Indians, Blackfeet, Chipewyans, Slave Indians, Crows, Flatheads, &c. Of these, the Crees are the quietest; they inhabit the woody country surrounding Hudson Bay, dwell in tents, never

---

[5] 'Hudson Bay.' R. M. Ballantyne

go to war, and spend their time in trapping, shooting, and fishing. The other tribes named above inhabit the vast plains and forests in the interior, on the east and west of the Rocky Mountains, and live chiefly by the produce of the chase.

NORTH AMERICAN INDIAN

The Indian walks with a long and stately stride, and his black eyes are restless from the habit he has acquired of always looking about in the forest in quest of game. His coarse black hair hangs in matted locks about his bead, and only in the hard winter does he wear any head-covering. Most of the men have now learned from the English to wear a coarse blue-striped cotton shirt, and a sort of loose coat of grey cloth in summer, which they change for a coat of deerskin in the winter. Their wives make them beautiful *leggins*, and *mocassins* for their feet of this same skin, ornamented with beads and dyed porcupine quills. Summer or winter, they seldom go out without a blanket over their shoulders. Nothing can be drearier than the long night marches of the Indians over their frozen plains in search of game. North of the 60th parallel the ground is frozen throughout nearly the whole year.

The province called BRITISH COLUMBIA, which lies to the west of the Rocky Mountains, contains far more people than the whole of the wide fur-hunting territory. Gold-diggers have flocked there in great numbers, because gold has been discovered quite lately in the banks of the Fraser River, which flows through the province. The pleasant Vancouver Island which lies off the coast forms part of British Columbia. Its climate is something like that of the British Isles.

The large island of NEWFOUNDLAND is the only part of British North America which is not included in the "Dominion of Canada." It is full of barren mountains and lakes, and has a long, cold winter, but the summer is dry and very hot. Little is known of the interior, and all the settlements are on the coast. In one of the harbours, Heart's Content Bay, is the American end of the Atlantic cables, which cross the ocean from Ireland. The great business of the settlers is the catching, curing, and sending away of cod. The town of St. John, the capital, is full of the smell of this fish; the ships in the harbour are laden with cod which they will carry all over the world; and sheds in which the fish are dried surround the harbour. There is no such cod fishery in the world as off the banks, which lie under water to the south of the island. The warm waters of the Gulf Stream wash these banks, and the fish swarm into the warm, pleasant shelter they afford.

QUESTIONS ON THE MAP OF NORTH AMERICA.

1. What great range of mountains runs through the whole length of North America? Name two mountains in this range.
2. Name the range which runs parallel with the Rocky Mountains, but nearer the coast. Two mountains in this range.
3. Name a country between these ranges which belongs to Britain.
4. What gulf nearly divides the peninsula of California from the mainland?
5. What peninsula forms the north-west corner of North America? By what strait is America here divided from Asia?
6. What name is given to the whole of the northern part of North America, excepting this peninsula?
7. Name five lakes which form part of the southern boundary of the Dominion of Canada. What large rivers are they connected with?
8. Entering the estuary of this river, between the island of Newfoundland and the peninsula of Nova Scotia, what land have we on our right As we sail up the lakes, what land is on our right?
9. What great bay breaks into the Dominion of Canada?
10. In what cape does Greenland end? What European island lies off its eastern coast?
11. What waters bound Greenland on the east? On the west?
12. By what three oceans is North America washed? Name any islands in the Arctic.
13. Name any lakes in British North America which are not in the great chain of lakes belonging to the St. Lawrence?
14. What island lies off the west coast near where the boundary line of the "Dominion" ends?
15. What great republic occupies the centre of the continent, from ocean to ocean?
16. What mighty river drains the United States? Where do its tributaries rise? Name the longest of these. Name any others that are marked on the map. Into what gulf does this river empty itself?
17. Name three cities in the United States.
18. What mountain-chain is there to the east of the Mississippi valley?
19. Name the southern country of North America.
20. What mountain-ranges does Mexico lie between? Name a mountain in this country.
21. What great gulf here breaks into the land?
22. Name the two peninsulas which partly enclose this gulf, on the north and the south.
23. What is that part of the continent called which lies between North and South America?
24. What name is given to the land in the narrowest part?
25. What two oceans would be united by a canal out through this isthmus?
26. What islands partly shut in the Caribbean Sea? Name those marked on the map, in the order of their size.

LESSON XLVI.
SOUTH AMERICA.

THE great western mountain range is called the Andes in South America. Beginning at the north coast, these mountains traverse the republic of Colombia in three great ridges, until they reach the equator. There, in Ecuador, the country of the equator, they draw together, and its capital city, Quito, stands upon the tableland thus formed, at a height of about 9500 feet above the sea; all round this city the snow-clad Andes form a great square. Though in the hottest region of the earth, the city lies so high that it is pleasantly cool, and about it are volcanoes which every now and then throw out flames that rise fully half a mile into the air. Among this bodyguard of mighty mountains are Chimborazo, Cotopaxi, and Antisana, all nearly 20,000 feet in height.

Further south, the Andes divide again into two chains, enclosing the high tablelands of Peru and Bolivia; thence to the south they form a single chain, in which is Aconcagua, the highest of the Andes.

Before describing the great central plain, we must notice two countries on the north coast—Venezuela, or "little Venice," which is oddly named, as it is a country twice as large as France; and Guiana, which is interesting to us, as part of it is BRITISH GUIANA, where much sugar is grown.

South America, as well as the northern continent, has mountains on its eastern side besides the great western range, and between these mountain ranges, from the north to the south of the continent, stretches an immense plain.

This plain has three great rivers flowing through it, and the plain of each of the rivers has a different character.

The plains of the northern river, the Orinoco, near 5° N. lat., are called *Savannahs*. In the dry season they are all parched up; there is not a green thing to be seen, hardly a living creature; the very ground opens in great dry cracks. The rains come, the river overflows; the plain is covered all at once with thick turf which presently grows tall like the prairie grass, and live things swarm in the air and on the ground.

Just on the equator flows out the Amazon, the mightiest of all the rivers, which, gathering many great tributaries as it goes, flows right across the continent from the mountains on the west. This river passes in its lower course through the *Selvas*, or forest plains, where the trees grow thick, and the forests are filled with underwood, and are bright with flowers, both upon the trees and upon the creeping plants which twine among them; where the mother monkeys play with their young ones, and where are the most beautiful birds, and beetles, and butterflies to be seen in the world.

This river flows through Peru and Brazil, two large countries which are famous for the gold and silver and diamonds found in their mountains and washed from the beds of their rivers.

It was the gentle, hospitable people of Peru who met with so cruel a fate from the Spaniards and Portuguese.

The plains of the third great river, which is indeed two rivers, the Parana and the Paraguay, flowing into the estuary of the La Plata, are called Pampas. The part between 30° and 40° S. is very remarkable: for nine months in the year, this whole district, right away to the mountains, is so overgrown with thistles, higher than the tallest man, that it is impossible to pass through it.

Other parts of the Pampas are covered with coarse grass, amongst which roam great herds of wild horses and cattle. The Gauchos, as the dwellers on the Pampas are called, capture these by means of a lasso, which is a long leather strap, more than twenty feet long, with a running noose at the end. The Gaucho gallops over the plain, and casts this noose over the head of the horse he wishes to capture.

On the west of the river is La Plata, which is named after the estuary. "Rio de la Plata" means river of silver, as much silver is washed from its bed. Two States on the east are named Paraguay and Uruguay, after the two rivers which form the estuary.

Patagonia, the southern country, is also a plain; for the most part stony and barren and very cold in the south. It is inhabited by men who live by hunting.

QUESTIONS ON THE MAP OF SOUTH AMERICA.

1. Between what oceans does South America lie?
2. What sea washes its north-western coasts?
3. By what isthmus is this continent joined to Central America?
4. Name four countries bordering the north-west coast.
5. What rivers drain the north-west corner of the continent?
6. What immense river crosses the country further south? Name three of its tributaries.
7. What great mountain chains run through the length of South America?
8. Name three countries which lie more or less between the parallel chains of the Andes.
9. Name a mountain in Chili.
10. Name a lake in Peru.
11. What large country occupies the valley of the Amazons?
12. Name two towns in Brazil.
13. Are there any mountains in South America besides the Andes? What country are they in?
14. Name two rivers which flow between these eastern mountain ranges.
15. What great river enters the ocean to the south of Brazil?
16. Name the three States drained by it.
17. What name is given to the district west of this river?
18. What is the most southern State of the continent called?
19. In what does it end? What strait divides this island from the mainland?
20. What cape forms the southern point of the island?
21. Name any other capes on the coast of South America.
22. What islands lie to the north-east of Cape Horn?
23. Name half-a-dozen important towns in South America, and say to what State each belongs.
24. What are the three great rivers of South America? In what direction do they all flow?
25. Name the countries of South America in the order of their size.
26. About how long is South America? How broad at the broadest part?

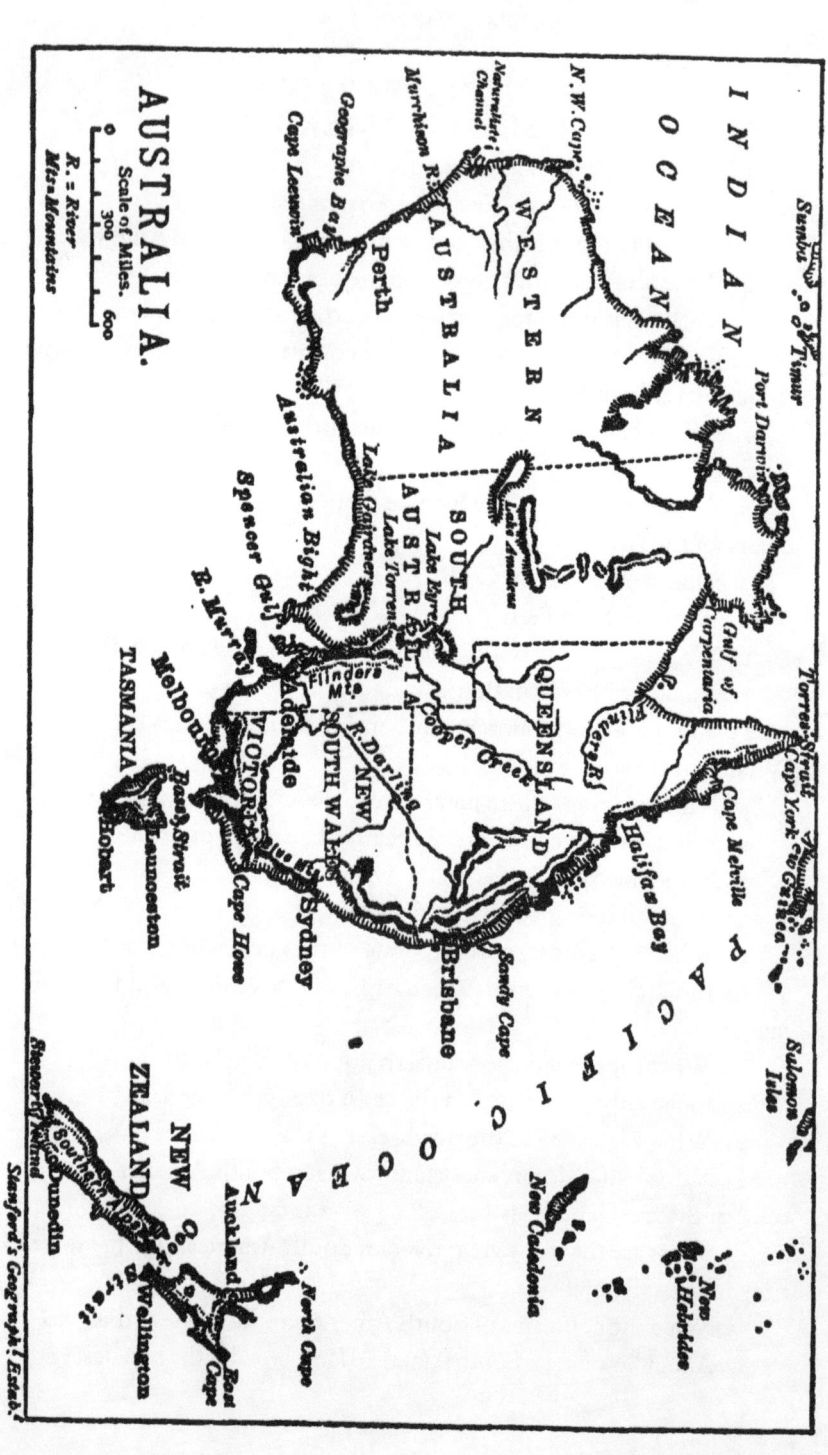

LESSON XLVII.
THE GREAT SOUTH LAND.

THE excitement and joy caused by the discovery of America led other navigators to imagine they also might be happy enough to find a new continent.

They consulted such maps of the world as had then been made, and saw that there was nothing but ocean marked to the south and east of Asia. As there was so much known land in the northern hemisphere, it seemed probable that a great south land might lie somewhere in these waters, and many went in search of such a continent. One of these, a Portuguese, it is supposed, was successful. He discovered the great south land which was named Australia.

But Australia did not prove so rich and inviting a land as America, and many years passed before settlers made their homes there. Indeed, for a long time it was only used as a place of punishment for English prisoners. At last people found out that they might grow rich by rearing sheep in Australia, to supply the English mills with wool; and later still it was discovered that in certain places, lumps, or nuggets, of gold might be found by lucky diggers.

Shiploads of emigrants from England and other countries are now carried over the ocean every year to settle in Australia. Most of these go to the south-east corner, which you will see is the only part of the map thickly marked with towns.

The Murray is the only large river in the whole of Australia, and even this sometimes dries up and becomes a chain of stagnant ponds; its large tributary, the Darling, however, flows constantly; it drains the south-east of the island. Mountains, with difficult passes, run close to the east and southeast coasts. In other parts, the coast is rock-bound, and there are few large openings. For these, and other reasons, it is very difficult to penetrate into Australia.

The whole island belongs to England, and when the emigrant lands at Sydney he might think he was in an English town. He hears none but English voices, sees English faces, and English-looking houses and streets. But outside the town he may find himself among great groves of orange trees laden with golden fruit; or may see peaches growing in such quantities that they are given to the pigs.

Towards the Blue Mountains, he comes upon forests of dull evergreen, or rather, ever grey, trees, whose narrow leaves turn edgewise to the sun, and cast but little shade. Now and then the dulness is enlivened by flocks of chattering parroquets and other birds of gorgeous plumage, crimson, green, and gold.

BLUE MOUNTAINS.

On the mountain slopes, be may come across the kangaroo, which bears its young in a pouch, and cannot walk or run, but gets over the ground with a curious spring.

He may chance on a colony of diggers, too, for gold is to be found all along these eastern mountains, and in the beds of the little rivers which flow from them.

On the inland slopes of the mountains are great pastures of grass (which grows in tufts, showing the earth between), with countless flocks of sheep upon them. These wide pastures, dotted with many flocks, stretch far into the interior, and as their flocks increase, the farmers move further and further inland.

The climate of Australia does better for rearing sheep than for growing corn. There are long seasons of drought when no rain falls, and then, in the wet season, sheets of water come down all at once until the streets of the towns look like rivers. As Australia is in the southern hemisphere, the seasons there are just the reverse of our own. Our summer is their winter, the wet season of Australia, and their Christmas Day comes in bright summer weather when it is nearly too hot to be out of doors; at least, it would be too hot anywhere else, but in Australia the heat is generally pleasant. Many travellers have laboured to explore the interior of Australia, and some of these have been lost. Those who have returned bring word that there is a good deal of sandy desert and a good deal of stony desert in the interior, but among these wastes are patches of pasture land. The three settlements on the east, New South Wales, Victoria, and Queensland, are all busy and prosperous; their chief towns, Sydney, Melbourne, and Brisbane, have wide, straight streets and handsome public buildings, and are in every way fine English towns.

Much of South Australia is unexplored, but there is little doubt that by far the larger part of it is occupied by dry, bare steppes. The most valuable part of this colony lies along the Flinders range of mountains, which extends from the eastern side of Spencer Gulf northwards towards the salt lakes Torrens and Eyre. These hills contain gold, silver, and copper; along their slopes, wheat, the vine, and other fruits are cultivated; and wide pasture lands surround this hill country. Adelaide is the capital city. Sheep are reared in Western Australia, but of this part of the continent but little is yet known.

Much of the rest of Australia is a wilderness, where the bare soil is encrusted with salt, and often covered with impenetrable thickets of a kind of prickly acacia; the little water channels or "creeks" dry up in the summer, and the animals search for standing pools. These deserts are not even inhabited by the aborigines.

The pleasant island of TASMANIA lies off the southeast corner of Australia, from which it is divided by Bass Strait. Its climate is like that of England, and where the island is cultivated, its villages and orchards and hedged fields remind one of the "mother country." The people are of British origin.

NEW ZEALAND.

AT a distance of about 1200 miles south-east of the mainland of Australia lie the islands of New Zealand. They are nearly at the antipodes of our island of Great Britain, that is, a line drawn through the centre of the globe from England would come out near them on the other side of the world. The group consists of two large islands, a northern and a southern, and of several smaller ones. The extent of the islands together is somewhat less than that of the United Kingdom.

Both islands are mountainous, and both have many rivers and lakes; the climate is like that of the British Isles. Forests of lofty pines and other evergreen trees, tree ferns and vegetation matted together by the rope-like *smilax*, occupy a large share of North, and some parts of South Island. Other parts are overgrown with ferns breast high, and others are well adapted for pasture.

Though New Zealand has no native quadrupeds, the plains of South Island are now so well stocked with sheep that wool has become one of the chief exports of the colony. The northern and eastern districts of South Island are those best fitted for agriculture, and here wheat, oats, and barley are grown.

New Zealand is very rich in minerals; in both islands gold-digging is carried on, and iron and coal are also found in South Island.

When these islands were first discovered by Captain Cook, they were peopled by the *Maoris*, a most handsome and intelligent people. A long-continued war was carried on during the years in which the British took possession of and settled in these islands, and the brave Maories are now greatly reduced in numbers; those who are left live peaceably in North Island chiefly, but the colonists are six or seven times as numerous. The chief towns are Wellington, Auckland, and Dunedin. The islands belong to England and are ruled by a British Governor.

POLYNESIA.

THE name Polynesia, or "many islands," is given to the numerous small islands and groups of islets in the Pacific. Some of these are mountainous, and these have usually been upheaved from the bottom of the sea; that is, they are of volcanic formation, and many of them still contain active volcanoes which belch out flame, ashes, and molten lava. The Society Isles in the centre of the South Pacific are volcanic. Tahiti, the largest of this group, is famous for its beautiful mountains, valleys, and cascades.

The Sandwich Islands, by far the most important to the north of the equator, are also volcanic. There are eight larger islands in the group, and in Hawaii, which is the largest island in mid-ocean, there are large volcanoes, and the *crater* (or opening) of one of these is like a lake of fire. The natives of the Sandwich Islands have a king or queen of their own, and are for the most part Christians. Honolulu, their capital city, is quite a handsome town.

The low islands of the Pacific have a very curious history; in this ocean, a little animal called the coral-polyp makes for itself a hard stony skeleton out of the tiny atoms of life which it draws from the sea-water. As millions of these polyps grow together, one stony skeleton branching out of another, they form great reefs of solid rook which sometimes appear above the water as islands, and sometimes barely rise to the water's edge. This is the case in the Great Barrier Reef of Australia, on which the swell of the ocean breaks continually, forming a long line of white foam, while the sea within the barrier is calm and still. This reef, which skirts the north-eastern coast for a length of more than 1200 miles, is the

CORAL ISLAND.

longest coral belt in the world. But the coral islands are generally round, consisting of a low reef in the form of a ring, and, in the centre, a blue lagoon, or lake of salt water, connected with the ocean by one or two openings. The reef is generally fringed with palm trees, and the whole island is more lovely than you can imagine. Such islands are called atolls.

But all the islands of Polynesia are beautiful; they lie within the torrid zone, and receive much moisture from the ocean, so are green and fertile and full of glowing flowers and fruits. The coco-palm affords the principal food of the people; but the breadfruit, yam, sweet potato, banana, coffee, sugar, and rice, all flourish in these happy isles. The natives manage their canoes well, and are in some of the islands a merry race, delighting to adorn themselves with the beautiful flowers their island homes produce. New Guinea, or Papua, is the largest island in all Polynesia—indeed it is five times as large as England and Wales. The country is almost covered with dense forests in which are many kinds of birds of the most gorgeous and beautiful plumage. The few natives live in small villages.

QUESTIONS ON THE MAP OF AUSTRALIA.

1. Between what oceans does Australia lie?
2. Name the five divisions of the island. Which is the largest? Which is the least populous?
3. The only large river is in the south-east; name it. What is its large tributary called?
4. In what parts of Australia are there mountains? Name those of New South Wales and of South Australia.
5. Name three or four large lakes in South Australia.
6. Give the chief towns of each of the four provinces on the east and south-east.
7. A town in Western Australia.
8. A large gulf in the north. What river flows into it?
9. A smaller gulf in the south.
10. Name the capes and bays round the coast.
11. Where is the Australian Bight?
12. What island is divided from Australia by Base Strait?
13. Name a town in this island.
14. What lands does Torres Strait separate?
15. Name three groups of islands in the Pacific, a thousand miles or so to the north-east of Australia. A large island to the north.
16. Two large distant islands to the south-east.
17. What strait divides North Island from South Island?
18. Name two towns in North Island. Two capes on its coasts.
19. A town in South Island.
20. A range of mountains in South Island.
21. Name the small island which forms quite the south of New Zealand.
22. About how long is New Zealand? How broad?
28. State roughly the length and breadth of Australia at its longest and broadest parts.

www.ingramcontent.com/pod-product-compliance
Lightning Source LLC
LaVergne TN
LVHW041955060526
838200LV00002B/24